THE
LEGACY OF
Pierre Teilhard de Chardin

Edited by James Salmon, SJ, and John Farina

PAULIST PRESS
New York/Mahwah, NJ

Cover and book design by Lynn Else

Library of Congress Cataloging-in-Publication Data

The legacy of Pierre Teilhard de Chardin / edited by James Salmon and John Farina.
    p. cm.
Includes bibliographical references.
ISBN 978-0-8091-4682-6 (alk. paper)
1. Teilhard de Chardin, Pierre. I. Salmon, James F. II. Farina, John.
B2430.T374L385 2011
194—dc22

2010029155

Published by Paulist Press
997 Macarthur Boulevard
Mahwah, New Jersey 07430

www.paulistpress.com

Printed and bound in the
United States of America

Contents

Preface
John Farina

My first encounter with Teilhard was in 1968 when I picked up a copy of *The Divine Milieu*. I was a high school student with a taste for theology. The title sounded interesting, and the abstract art on the cover caught my eye. I didn't understand a thing.

How could I? Teilhard begins the essay with a quote from St. Paul: "No man lives to himself. Whether we live or whether we die, we are the Lord's." Teilhard tells us the whole work is nothing more than an explication of those words. Eighteen-year-olds usually don't know much about dying.

Teilhard did. He was a scientist who studied dead things. Things from very long ago that survived only in fossils, rock, and bones, things long dead that only a skilled eye could tell were once alive.

Teilhard was not only a scientist but a profound religious thinker. His spirituality came out of his various experiences as a Jesuit, a student of paleontology, and a twentieth-century man. The Jesuit influences are plain to see. Ignatius taught his followers to discern the action of God in their own mental operations and in external events. Profoundly, God is working in our imagination, our will, our affections, and our understanding. More and more we can learn to become aware of his working, and that awareness can enable us to make decisions and take actions that advance

God's kingdom on earth. We can learn in every situation to find what is better and to act to advance it.

For Teilhard that was true not only of us but of all creation: "By means of all created things, without exception, the divine assails us."[1] "Without exception." A terrifying thought. Death and destruction, suffering and darkness, violence, even entropy itself, all are working together for good. Sanctification is to be worked in us through the created order. If we awake from our stupor, we can see, like Jacob rising from his dream of angels descending and ascending to heaven, that we are truly in a holy place, because all the cosmos is the divine milieu.

It, however, takes enlightened eyes to see the divine milieu, because it assembles and harmonizes within itself qualities that appear contradictory. Vast and intricate, full of countless arrays of creatures, it nevertheless can appear near, tangible, even comforting. God reveals himself as that milieu. He is the ultimate point upon which all realities converge, the center that fills the sphere, which, as the Scholastics were fond of saying, has a circumference that is everywhere.

Yet this is not the God of the pantheist. The omnipresence of the divine is the effect of God's spirituality and the exact opposite of the ubiquity that matter seems to derive from its extreme dispersal in the universe. This vast milieu, however large, is a center with the absolute power to unite all things in itself. It does not unite things into a monad. Individual beings do not lose their uniqueness. In the milieu all the elements of the universe touch each other by that which is most inward and ultimate in them. Like the souls in Dante's *Paradiso* who are most fully themselves when they finally are united to God in the beatific vision, so too are duality and difference preserved in the divine milieu. Pantheism presents a vision of union, but ultimately offers only a destiny of fusion and unconsciousness. On the contrary, in the divine milieu, the elect discover in God the consummation of their individual fulfillment.

On the surface we experience desolation when we observe the losses, the separations, the deaths of things within our horizon. We see only the surface, however. Without leaving this world, but precisely in the midst of it, we plunge into God: "There and from there, in Him and through Him, we shall hold all things and have command of all things."[2] There we shall find again all the things we have lost and despaired of ever having again. Teilhard felt this keenly. Physical diminishment, illness, sickness, and death were only forces whose purpose was to work a greater will, to return us to the universe, the divine milieu that had given us substance and formed us. All the ill fortune we sustain, the opposition of others, the malignity of disease, the deterioration of our faculties, form what Teilhard called, following Ignatius, our internal passivities. Passivities are not merely external. Sooner or later, we all come to realize that a process of ultimate disorganization and diminution has installed itself deep within our bodies. Death will conquer us all in the end: "In death, as in an ocean, all our slow or swift diminishments flow out and merge. Death is the sum and consummation of all our diminishments: it is evil itself—pure physical evil, in so far as it results organically from the material plurality in which we are immersed—but moral evil too, insofar as this disordered plurality, the course of all strife and all corruption, is engendered in society or in ourselves by the wrong use of our liberty."[3] We must overcome death by finding God in it. Our activities are divinized. Our passivities are divinized. All endeavor cooperates to complete the world in Christ. In action we commune with Christ. In our passivities we likewise commune with Christ. Through diminishment we resign ourselves to God's will, and in that resignation find peace and wonderment.

Teilhard's sense of wonder permeated all he did; many thought him a wonder. A scientist who wrote like a poet, with the heart of a mystic. It is no surprise men like Arnold Toynbee, Julian Huxley, Andre Malraux, Gustav Weigel, SJ, John LaFarge, SJ, and many other of his contemporaries sang his praises. They called him "the new Galileo," "the Thomas Aquinas of our age," "the equal of Teresa of Avila or John of the Cross."[4] All of this made Teilhard a star. His books were published around the world by major secular houses. His appeal went far beyond the "Catholic ghetto" to the mainstream media. His *Mass on the World* was set to music and a recording released. Other composers followed suit and recorded albums of new compositions inspired by Teilhard's vision of humanity evolving to a higher consciousness.

Interest in his work reached a crescendo in the mid-1960s, at a time when his rapprochement with the new science of evolution seemed but one more sign of just how well the church could fit into the modern world. His cosmic optimism also fit well an age when humanity, for a brief, shining moment after the destruction of the Second World War, hoped that international cooperation and enlightened respect for life could advance civilization to a new level of development. Then came the social upheavals of the late 1960s. Concern for questions of civil rights, peace, justice, and the church's role in international affairs pushed aside the questions Teilhard grappled with. His optimism seemed out of joint with the grim landscape of war, protest, injustice, and struggle that dominated the sixties.

But that age is now past, although it dies hard. This book, therefore, is written for a new generation, one for whom the sixties have taken their place in the long roll of decades past. Why might new eyes, living in a postmodern world, look upon Teilhard with new interest?

Postmodernity, whatever else it might do, prides itself in challenging metanarratives. There is, correspondingly, a new openness to personal narrative, to contradiction, chaos, randomness, and diversity. Teilhard's narrative of the divine milieu is, to be sure, grand. He addresses the largest questions of human origin and destiny. Yet, he does so by placing them in the drama of the universe, a drama whose scope is so vast and complex that it constantly baffles efforts to capture it in any one system of thought. Grand narratives fade when heard over the course of billions of years. The mind's ability to construct such theories is staggered by gazing at but a tiny corner of the universe, and an experience of *mysterium tremendum* is the only response.

Teilhard takes up the life of the cosmos and hints at how we are lost in it, though strangely comforted in the end by the thing in which all things consist. This is just the note many listeners today will hear in Teilhard's music. The contradiction, the tension, the paradox, and mystery—always at the heart of religion—are freed from the shackles of ordinary expectations to confront us afresh. Set in the context of the life of the cosmos, the traditional questions of theology take on a new tone.

Postmodernity's suspicion of metanarrative also has taken its toll on popular perceptions of science. Gone is the confidence of the mid-twentieth century that science will ensure steady and unmitigated progress for humanity. The positivism that was still present in Teilhard's day has been humbled by keener understandings of the epistemological basis of scientific theory and by the perduring of intractable social problems. As a result, the old hostilities between science and religion, while not gone, increasingly appear as modern relics. Through all of this Teilhard's science and mysticism can be read with a new openness and credulity.

Introduction

James Salmon, SJ

Teilhard's Relevance for Today

In a 2007 message to the American Teilhard Association, Kofi Annan, then secretary general of the United Nations, wrote about the significance of Teilhard's thought for his predecessors Dag Hammarskjold, U Thant, and Javier Peres de Cuellar: "Finally, I am convinced that Pere Teilhard de Chardin is a thinker for the twenty-first century."[1]

Who was Teilhard de Chardin? And why, even today, is his thought still significant? Teilhard, geologist and Jesuit, wanted to know what evolution has told us about our ancestors, about Jesus Christ, about the future. Early in his scientific career he began to wonder about such questions, and spent the remainder of his life trying to find answers that made sense to himself and to others. Is there any possible way that ancient faith can be reconciled with what today's science reveals? Now, more than fifty years since his death, as issues of faith and science continue to remain at the forefront of political, religious, and academic discussion, we can acknowledge that Teilhard's insights shed light on humanity's place and purpose. At the least, they deserve a hearing.

Teilhard had a unique career. In the 1920s he was well known in Parisian intellectual salons for his ideas about God, Christ, and evolution, ideas that are still relevant today. Yet his name disappeared, and did not reappear again publicly in Paris until he returned from China in 1946. In the meantime he had acquired a worldwide reputation, but within a relatively small community of thinkers who had scientific interests similar to his own. When he returned to post–World War II France and began to speak publicly again, he quickly became, along with Jean Paul Sartre, one of the two most sought-after lecturers in Paris. But he suddenly left France again in 1950 without a published legacy of the ideas that had made his talks so popular. He died in New York City in 1955, relatively unknown, except to some close friends and a small international community of scientists.

Teilhard's ideas underwent a revival in the 1960s, when many young people became familiar with his name after his literary legacy outside of science was collected and published in seventeen languages. During that troubled period, his worldwide vision offered hope and enthusiasm for the future of humanity. In 1964 Henry R. Luce, the editor of *Life* magazine, headed a full-page editorial about Teilhard, "A Great Thinker's Joyful Vision: the Spiritual Perfection of Mankind."[2]

In the 1970s his popularity began to wane. New generations with a more practical bent emerged, and his admirers of the sixties generation became older, concerned now with practical matters like family, taxes, and jobs. Essays and books about Teilhard continued to appear in bookstores but on a more limited scale. However, when worldwide publishers Harper and Collins conducted a recent survey of the one hundred most important spiritual books published in the twentieth century, Teilhard's *The Phenomenon of Man* (more properly translated as *The Human Phenomenon*) was found to be number one.

Increasingly, people today are aware of what science reveals about human origins. Many wonder if evolution is compatible with the ancient wisdom passed down through generations and the assertion of most world religions that human existence is meaningful. A few contemporary scientists argue, based on the nature of the universe, that human existence is essentially meaningless. Teilhard, as these essays demonstrate, thought otherwise.

Teilhard's Legacy and Life

Born in 1881 in the French province of Auvergne, Teilhard was the fourth of eleven children. He writes of the serious interest of his father in the study of nature and his mother's deep Christian piety as important factors in family life. He entered the Jesuit order in 1899. Thomas King describes the importance of Teilhard's Jesuit novice director's advice that set the course for his future life as scientist and missionary. Teilhard later wrote that whereas St. Paul spoke to the Areopagites at Athens of "an unknown God," like St. Paul, Teilhard found his vocation in life to show others how dark adoration of their world could become the luminous gleam of the risen Christ. In a recently published Jesuit yearbook, historian John W. O'Malley wrote how the image of Teilhard de Chardin digging away at archaeological sites in China is quintessentially Jesuit, a reflection of the commitment of the Society of Jesus to its cultural mission within a religious framework.

Theologian John Haught affirms and shows the religious significance of Teilhard's being the first to propose a scientific law of complexity-consciousness, that evolution indicates humans are only part of the way toward the goal of evolution. Like Teilhard, Haught contends that evolution is absolutely essential to understand an intensely purposeful universe.

While assigned to teaching in a Jesuit high school in Cairo, Egypt, Teilhard had the opportunity to communicate the vitality of his interest in natural history by taking his students on field expeditions. The result of this hunt for fossils, minerals, and rare insects was his first scientific research paper published in 1909. After studies in theology and ordination to the priesthood, he was asked to contribute to an encyclopedia an essay on the theology of miracles. Paleontologist Mark McMenamin appraises this essay within the history of science. As far as it is known, Teilhard never referred to or spoke about this article again. McMenamin goes on to inquire about miracles such as those at Lourdes that are verified by many witnesses, including scientists and physicians. He asks why these miracles are not acceptable as phenomena to be investigated by tools of science.

Teilhard went on to study the sciences of geology and paleontology at the Paris Museum from 1912 until 1914, when he was inducted into the French army. For four years he participated in many of the bloodiest battles of World War I. Letters to his cousin and confidant, Marguerite Teillard Chambon, during this period describe regular contact with death and the experience of fierce trench warfare for which that war is known. Teilhard turned down a battlefield promotion to be an officer in order to remain as stretcher carrier with his Algerian regiment. During this period, he was decorated for gallantry on the battlefield with the highest honors of the French Republic. It was also during this period that he began to write down his ideas in copybooks, *cahiers*, which contain the seeds of his vision.

Ewert Cousins situates the theme of World Soul in Teilhard's vocabulary that was introduced by Thomas King. Cousins discusses the compatibility of Teilhard's early writings during World War I with historical Christian doctrines of World Soul. The doctrines are foundational principles of the cosmic theology of Greek fathers of the Christian Church, and of Western medieval theologians. Cousins describes why Teilhard became disillusioned with the Scholasticism that he had learned in the seminary, and why he is often identified now with a neo-Platonic and Franciscan theological tradition. A valuable manifestation of Cousins' thesis is a small volume, *My Conversations with Teilhard de Chardin on the Primacy of Christ*, written by Franciscan scripture scholar, Gabriel M. Allegra.[3]

After World War I Teilhard returned to the Sorbonne, where in 1922 he defended his doctoral dissertation in geology. His thesis director, Marcellin Boule, noted ten years later on the occasion of Teilhard's receiving a distinguished award for the quality of the dissertation:

> He…possesses every quality required of a first-rate naturalist; an aptitude for work, penetrating observa-

tion, a combination—valuable as it is rare—of keen-
ness for minute analysis and a gift for wide synthesis,
and great independence of mind. His career, though
just begun, already gives promise of being among the
most brilliant.[4]

At the time of a jubilee celebration for Boule, Teilhard was
delegated to speak. He asked the famous professor:

Do you remember our first interview about the middle
of July in 1912?…About two that afternoon I timidly
approached to ring the bell at the door—since so often
entered—on the Place Valhubert.…And I began what
has been my life ever since.[5]

Because of the quality of his early scientific publications,
Teilhard was selected to teach geology at the Institute Catholique
de Paris, and in 1923 was elected president of the Société
Géologique de Paris. At the time he was also selected as paleontologist to set up the French Paleontological Mission in China.
During the time in China, while conducting research in geology
and paleontology in the field, he began a draft of what was to
become later his *Mass on the World*.

An important event in Teilhard's scientific career was his
appointment in 1929 as official advisor to the director of the
China Geological Survey. The appointment gave him the opportunity to help plan and carry out scientific programs that
explored the whole Asian continent. His collaboration with the
best Chinese and expatriate members of the research community
manifested his rare qualities as both skilled field geologist and
keen theoretician, qualities seldom found together in scientists.
In his official capacity he was able to exert considerable influence
on the research. It is written that his charm also inspired a spirit
of collaboration. As one geoscientist-collaborator, Helmut de

Terra, wrote, "Father Teilhard was my friend, the most cherished and revered human being I ever met."[6]

During the China period Teilhard formulated and developed what is called by philosophers of science his scientific research program. Ludovico Galleni describes for the first time in non-technical language the essentials of the origin of this research program, and its unique relationship with Teilhard's religious perspective. Galleni's familiarity both with Teilhard's correspondence with other scientists and with eleven volumes of Teilhard's published scientific research permits him to describe why Teilhard was able to yoke together a research program that includes his religious and scientific perspectives about an emerging universe.

The China period was also a special time during which Teilhard reflected directly on the implications of his religious faith. During this period he was asked by a friend to portray in writing something of his theological vision. Theologian, author, and editor Philip Hefner explains the spiritual and theological significance of the key essay, "My Universe," in order to understand Teilhard's spiritual perspective. The vision recognizes the materiality of the human spiritual journey. For Teilhard the study of matter and nature is revelatory of God, not unlike the psalmists. Moreover, an evolutionary vision can direct one's moral striving toward building the earth, a contribution to the process that Teilhard called Christogenesis.

Beginning in 1915 and until his death, Teilhard regularly put down his thoughts, principally about his own philosophical and theological reflections and ideas, in his private handwritten copybooks or *cahiers*. These notes are invaluable because they became the seeds to develop essays he would write later. One can trace in them developments of his thinking over periods of time. Most of the essays were not published until after his death because of a ban by church superiors in 1926 of publication of his essays concerned with philosophy or theology. Teilhard obeyed their decision until he died in 1955. When he returned to Europe at the close of World War II he left the copybooks behind in China with the intention of returning there. Unfortunately, because of political changes in China after the war, he was unable to return. Serious efforts have been made by French and Chinese governments to recover the copybooks between 1925 and 1945, but they have never been found.

As editors of eleven volumes of Teilhard's scientific work, and because of their familiarity with Teilhard's thought, Nicole Schmitz-Moormann and her late husband Karl were selected by Teilhard's family to edit the remaining private handwritten copybooks and other materials concerned with his thought that have been collected. Thirty-five years of editing permits Nicole Schmitz-Moormann for the first time to write down and enlighten us with her unique familiarity with principal themes in Teilhard's literary legacy.

Back in Paris after World War II, Teilhard was treated as a celebrity. His reputation was based on both his scientific accomplishments and some of his essays that friends had mimeographed and circulated. In a post–World War II culture in France, his vision and the hope it incorporated made him a most attractive speaker. James Skehan portrays some of the scientific and spiritual accomplishments that warranted Teilhard's reputation. Skehan was finishing his doctoral work in geology at Harvard when he met Teilhard, who was visiting some old friends on the Harvard faculty. Since that time Skehan has become a leading geologist in his own right. Like Teilhard, Skehan is both a Jesuit priest and a geologist. He writes with insight into Teilhard the priest, scientist, and mystic.

Based on his scientific talent and experience, Teilhard was elected to the French Academy of Sciences, and it was proposed in 1948 by authorities at the College of France that he fill the chair in Geology there. Although aware that the College of France would unanimously vote for him, church authorities disapproved of such an appointment because his ideas about religion and philosophy were ahead of his time. They decided it would be better for all concerned if he left France permanently. As a result, he finally took up residence in New York City.

From the earliest days of his professional training as a scientist, Teilhard struggled with the question, Why are other planets in our solar system barren and yet evolution takes place on the Earth? He labeled the heading of part IV of his original *Le phénomène humain*, "Survival," since he was so aware of the issue. Teilhard was one of the very few scientists who are known to have thought seriously about this scientific enigma, including the origin of life and the appearance of new species on planet Earth. Throughout his career he wondered why the process of evolution on Earth seemed to contradict laws of science. The validity of his struggle and his proposed ambiguous solution to the question is explained in the reprint of a recent publication in *Zygon: Journal of Religion and Science*. As Harold Morowitz, Nicole Schmitz-Moormann, and James Salmon show, Teilhard's intuition about two energies in the universe, tangential and radial energies, was prescient if one takes into consideration the emergence of our more recent understanding of modern science and information theory.

Since he had to leave France permanently, Teilhard was invited to direct a study of human origins for the Wenner-Gren Foundation in New York City. He made extended visits to Africa in 1951 and 1953, where, among other activities, he helped to establish a network of research throughout the world. He died suddenly in New York City on Easter Sunday, 1955. It is revealing that a month before his death he expressed the wish to some friends that he might die "on the day of the Resurrection."[7]

It is hoped that this book may promote acceptance and discussion by theologians and philosophers of the reality of evolution, and scientists may catch the gleams of light from a soaring mind that saw in the barren rocks and stony hieroglyphs of nature a spiritual message denied to lesser minds.

CHAPTER ONE

Teilhard, Cosmic Purpose, and the Search for Extraterrestrial Intelligence

John F. Haught

For many years my main academic and theological interest has been the relationship of science to religion.[1] I have come to the conclusion that when we get down to the very bottom of the many specific questions that surround this topic, the main issue is whether one can speak plausibly today of the universe as having some point, purpose, or meaning to it. Perhaps some readers are wondering why we should talk about this question at all. People are usually interested in the question of purpose or meaning in their own lives, but why would anybody care whether or not the universe as a whole has any point or meaning to it?

One very good reason to care is that modern science—biology, evolution, cosmology, and physics—has shown how intricately each of us is tied into the whole universe. We are inseparable from it. The American philosopher W. T. Stace says that if the whole universe is pointless, then so also are the individual lives tied to it. Not everybody would agree, but Vaclav Havel, the outgoing president of the Czech Republic, in several speeches while he was still president, said that "the crisis of the much needed global responsibility is due to the fact that we've lost the sense that the universe has a purpose."[2] And if you poll the religions of the world, they would agree, almost unanimously, that it is important, especially for the sake of sustaining moral aspiration from generation to generation, that people believe that the universe is here for a reason.

However, we live in an age of science, and for many people today, especially in the intellectual world, the question is: Can we reconcile the ageless religious belief that the universe is here for a reason with what the natural sciences are saying? Steven Weinberg has famously stated that "the more [scientifically] comprehensible the universe has become, the more pointless it also seems."[3] And Richard Feynman, another widely respected twentieth-century physicist, has stated: "The great accumulation of understanding as to how the physical world behaves, only convinces one that this behavior has a kind of meaninglessness about it."[4]

Yet compare these statements to what we might call the "Wisdom of the Ages," the great philosophical and religious traditions of humanity, all of which think of the universe as purposeful. For them the universe consists of a ladder of levels, moving from matter at the bottom through plant life, animal life, human consciousness, and sometimes intermediary realms of angelic beings, to Ultimate Reality and Meaning at the top. Each level receives its meaning by being taken up into a higher level, and that level into an even higher, until ultimately all are assumed into the life of God.

This scheme operates according to what I like to call the "hierarchical principle." This principle maintains that a higher level in any hierarchy can encompass or comprehend a lower, but a lower cannot comprehend or encompass the higher. And so, what this principle would mean for our understanding of science and religion today is that achieving cognitional competency at the lower levels does not necessarily qualify one to say anything about, or comment on, the higher levels. Almost unanimously, the great religions and philosophies thought that in order for us humans to be able to say anything about the higher levels, we would have to go through a process of personal transformation. Philosophy, at least for many centuries, required a discipline, an apprenticeship, or a set of exercises that allowed one to achieve *adaequatio*, that is adequacy or competency to understand the higher dimensions of reality. As E. F. Schumacher writes in *A Guide for the Perplexed* one must achieve *adaequatio* in order to be in a position to comment on whether the higher levels exist at all, or on what their nature might be. The Wisdom of the Ages teaches that the more important something is, the more elusive it is to human consciousness. And so, if there is an ultimate meaning or purpose to the universe, it would lie, by definition, beyond the comprehension of human consciousness. If there is an ultimate meaning it might comprehend us and our consciousness, but our consciousness could not comprehend, or wrap itself around, it.[5]

This does not mean, of course, that the ultimate level is unknowable in every sense. For we can have an awareness of being grasped by the ultimate. The theologian Paul Tillich defined faith as the state of being grasped by what one takes to be of ultimate concern. But we can never attain a grasping or comprehending understanding of any conceivable ultimate meaning. Absolute clarity would actually diminish our sense of the ultimate. So if there is any purpose to the universe, we can refer to it only by way of symbols, metaphors, and analogies. We cannot justifiably pretend ever to have a clear and distinct understanding of what the purpose of things is.

Now compare the classical hierarchical religious outlook to the contemporary scientific picture of the universe. The cosmos as portrayed by modern science is said, by the latest estimates, to be about 13.7 billion years old. You may picture the unfolding of the cosmic story in the following way. Imagine that you have thirty large books on your shelf, and each of those volumes is 450 pages long. Each page in each book stands for one million years. The Big Bang takes place on page one of volume 1. But the first twenty-two tomes consist of what seems from the scientific perspective to be essentially lifeless and mindless physical stuff. The

Earth's story begins in volume 21, four billion years ago. About a billion or so years later, in volume 22, the first sparks of life begin to flame up—3.8 billion years ago. Still, life is not in a hurry to become terribly complex until around the end of volume 29, where the famous Cambrian explosion takes place. Then, all of a sudden, the forms of life become much more interesting, at least from a human point of view. Even so, dinosaurs don't come in until after the middle of volume 30; and they go extinct on page 385, sixty-five pages from the end. The last sixty-five pages comprise the age of mammals, and eventually primates and humans. Our hominid ancestors arrive on the last several pages of volume 30. But modern humans do not appear until possibly the last fifth or so of the very last page of volume 30. That is when intelligence, ethical aspiration, and other features we associate with our humanity begin to burst onto the cosmic scene.

Now, if you are scientifically educated today, you cannot help asking: What is the point of this great epic? Is there a continuous thematic thread that ties together what is going on on page one of volume 1 with what happens on page 450 of volume 30? Apparently not, at least according to many scientific thinkers. It appears to the likes of Weinberg and Feynman that there is a kind of aimlessness to the process. If there is a "point" to the universe, there must be some kind of narrative continuity that ties the thirty volumes together into a meaningful whole. But, at least for many smart people today, it is hard to find such coherence.

Notice that the hierarchical cosmology that provided the backbone of traditional spirituality and the sense of purpose apparently gets flattened out by contemporary science—horizontalized, you might say. Life seems hard to distinguish from lifeless matter. In the new cosmic story, life emerges only gradually out of lifeless matter, and mind comes in apparently as a kind of cosmic afterthought. Finally, meaning, which was the highest level in the traditional hierarchy, seems—at least to modern and postmodern thought—to be nothing more than an illusion projected by the human mind onto the coldness of an impersonal cosmos.

As if the flattening of the hierarchy were not enough to squeeze purposiveness out of nature altogether, the ancient sense of reality has also been pulverized by another major development in modern thought: atomism. Atomism, the method of explaining complex things by breaking them down into their constituent particulars, has served to fragment the classic worldview into elemental pieces with no inherent significance. Atomism, of course, is an ancient temptation, associated especially with the pre-Socratic philosopher Democritus, who said that all one needs to understand reality are two concepts, atoms and the void. Democritean atomism went underground for a number of centuries because of the dominance of Platonism and Aristotelian thought, both of which gave to "form" or pattern an importance that atomism did not. But in modern times, especially with the birth of classical physics in the seventeenth century, and particularly with the particles-in-motion universe of Newton, atomism returned with a vengeance. And so, by the time the nineteenth century came along and Darwinian theory burst onto the scene, it became possible—as is true even to this day—for some evolutionists to interpret the story of life simply as a kind of reshuffling of the atomic elements that are said to make up the universe. This is the thrust of Daniel Dennett's book *Darwin's Dangerous Idea* (1995), for example.[6] In the 1950s atomism received a significant boost by way of the developments in molecular biology, which tries as far as possible to explain life and mind in terms of chains of atoms. And even more recently, atomism found a new partner in E. O. Wilson's sociobiology and the derivative fields of evolutionary anthropology and evolutionary psychology, which try to explain human behavior in terms of the drive of genes (segments of DNA taken to be the new atomic units) to get into the next generation.

Atomism, however, may be either a method or a philosophy. Methodological atomism, if I may call it that, is essential to science. Neuroscience, for example, rightly tries to explain mind as much as possible in terms of its atomic, molecular, cellular, and modular constituents. But a more philosophical atomism has also appeared in modern times, claiming that all things are ontologically reducible to atomic particulars. Teilhard refers to it as the "analytical illusion." It has arisen in the shadow of the modern Cartesian expulsion of mind from matter. Mind, according to Descartes and his followers, lies on one side of a sharp divide, and matter falls on the other. What this dualism has come to imply is that matter is *essentially mindless*. And once mind has thereby been exorcised from the realm of matter, this leaves only an atomized, mindless, and hence essentially purposeless universe as the remainder. It is on this imaginary universe of mindless stuff that modern cosmic pessimism has been so boldly established. Then, as if to add salt to the wound, beginning in the nineteenth century life itself has been assimilated into the mindless atomistic universe of modern cosmic pessimism. And by emphasizing the randomness, competitive struggle, and impersonality in life's evolution, Darwinian biology seems to many modern scientific thinkers to confirm the idea, once and for all, that we live in an essentially pointless universe. This cosmic pessimism is taken for granted in many popular scientific writings today, as well as in academic philosophy.

Teilhard and Cosmic Purpose

Before looking at Teilhard de Chardin's response to modern cosmic pessimism I should pause here and define more carefully what I mean by "purpose." Purpose, as I understand it, quite simply means *the realization of a value*. Any process that seems to be aiming toward or bringing about what is self-evidently good or valuable may be called purposive. We know from personal experience that what ties together the moments of our own lives, insofar as we think of our lives as meaningful, is the sense that somehow we are actualizing, or helping to bring about, something of value. Could it not be said, then, that any universe which

14

is in the process of realizing *mind* or *consciousness*, an undeniable value, is at the very least a purposive cosmos?

If the universe is to be purposeful, Teilhard argued, it has to have at least a loose kind of directionality to it. In other words, it has to be more than just aimlessly wandering around. And if anybody looks carefully at the evolution of life in the context of the whole cosmic unfolding, it is not hard to see that there clearly is an axis of directionality running through it. Moreover, this directionality is measurable. Its measurable side consists of the gradual increase in organized physical complexity in the course of cosmic history. As atoms become molecules, molecules become cells, and cells become organisms, the universe grows increasingly more complex in its organization. Then in the emergence of vertebrates, primates, and finally humans, nervous systems and brains become almost unimaginably complex in their organization.[7]

Furthermore, there is no reason to insist that evolution has now come anywhere near the end of its journey. If you look under your feet, behind your back, and over your head, you will see a new type of organized physical complexity now taking shape. Teilhard calls this latest evolutionary level of being the "noosphere," from the Greek word *nous*, which means "mind." The human phenomenon is now weaving itself collectively around our planet, taking advantage of politics, economics, education, scientific developments, and especially communication technology. Teilhard, incidentally, is sometimes called the "prophet of the Internet" because he predicted that through technological complexification the Earth would continue to clothe itself in something like a brain. The noosphere is so new by evolutionary standards that science does not yet know quite what to make of it. In evolution, after all, significant outcomes usually take millions upon millions of years, but the formation of the noosphere so far is a matter of only thousands, and especially of the last two hundred years. So we should not assume that the universe's aim toward more and more complex physical organization is at its end. Perhaps, for all we know, evolutionary creation is still at the cosmic dawn.[8]

Nevertheless, physical complexification in evolution is interesting to Teilhard primarily because, in direct proportion to the gradual increase in organized physical complexity, there is a corresponding increase in *consciousness*. Teilhard refers here to the "law of complexity-consciousness," which maintains that consciousness increases in direct proportion to the degree of increase in physical complexity. What's going on in the universe, at the very least, is a gradual increase in the intensity of consciousness. And this is enough to fill it with purpose, a notion that I defined earlier as the "realizing of a value." It is impossible to deny consistently that consciousness is a self-evident value, for if you find yourself denying it this can only be because you value your consciousness enough to make such a judgment. Since consciousness is clearly a value, a universe that is in the business of bringing about more and more intense versions of consciousness is an intensely purposeful universe.

Not only is there an increase in complexity and consciousness, there is also an intensification of freedom. The aim toward freedom is another trend that makes it possible to call the universe meaningful. But the increase of consciousness and freedom occurs only because of a deeper tendency of cosmic reality to organize itself around a center. "Centration" in cosmic history is already going on at the level of the atom, where the nucleus somehow organizes the subatomic elements. And centration continues at the level of the eukaryotic living cell with its well-defined nucleus. Centration becomes much more intense at the level of vertebrates with their complex central nervous systems. In primates centration intensifies further in the heightened consciousness made possible by a more complex brain. Then with humans centration reaches the state of self-awareness. Teilhard's point is that, by anybody's standards, in evolution there has been a discernible directional increase in centration and, along with it, an intensifying of inwardness or subjectivity.[9]

And now that the universe has reached the stage of the noosphere, what is the form that the search for the center takes?

The most characteristic way in which the search for the center—which has always been going on in the universe—continues now is that of *religion*. Religion fits into the evolutionary universe as the way in which conscious life carries on the search for a center. Most religions are in search of a higher reality or a supercenter, as Teilhard called it. And of course for Teilhard, who was a Christian theist, the name of this supercenter is God. Teilhard believed God has become incarnate in the Christ, and he understood Christ as the physical goal of *cosmic* evolution. But in all of religion the search for a center has been going on from the time of the earliest expressions of spiritual inquiry. Consequently, we should look at religion not only theologically, historically, psychologically, or sociologically, but also cosmologically. For Teilhard religion is the way in which the *universe*, now that it has reached the level of self-awareness, continues its ageless search for the Center. So religion, instead of being opposed to evolution, is absolutely essential to its future.

As Teilhard writes in *Activation of Energy*:

> What is most vitally necessary to the thinking earth is a faith and a great faith and ever more faith, to know that we are not prisoners, to know that there is a way out, that there is air and light and love somewhere beyond the reach of all death. To know this, to know that it is neither an illusion nor a fairytale, that if we are not to perish smothered in the very stuff of our being—this is what we must at all costs secure. And it is there that we find what I may well be so bold as to call the evolutionary role of religions.[10]

For the sake of the universe and its future we must cultivate and purify, not abandon, our religious traditions.

Finally, for Teilhard, the meaning of our own lives must also have something to do with our participation in the evolutionary process of complexification, socialization, centration—of searching for deeper freedom and increasing consciousness. Participating in evolution is often difficult and painful. But suffering and struggle are for Teilhard best understood as the dark side of an unfinished universe. Obviously, suffering is much more than that, but that is how it would fit into an evolving and still unperfected cosmos. Teilhard believes that in the end the struggle of life will have proven to be worth the effort. But, for anything significant to come of evolution as far as humans are concerned, henceforth each of us has to make some serious choices in our lives. He calls this set of choices the "Grand Option."[11]

First of all we have to decide between whether we want to live as pessimists or as optimists. If we choose the path of pessimism, including what I have been calling cosmic pessimism, this can only lead to an evolutionary dead end. Evolution on Earth will terminate tragically if we fall into a state of despair or pessimism about the future. But suppose you choose to live for the future? Suppose the horizon opens up ahead of you? Then you still have to make a choice as to what kind of future you are going to hope for. One option is to aspire to get out of this world altogether, as in some forms of traditional Christian spirituality. Teilhard refers to this option as the "optimism of withdrawal." It is a hope to get out of the mess we are in here, to leave the universe and the cosmos behind as soon as possible, so that we can find our true destiny elsewhere.

This is a very attractive and comforting option for millions of people. However, another horizon of hope has opened up because of science, and especially because of the arrival of evolutionary thought and new developments in cosmology. This alternative prospect is the "optimism of evolution." It is based on the sense that the universe is still not finished, still in the process of being created. So why should we not get excited about participating in the ongoing creation of this universe? The universe may still have a great future ahead of it. Teilhard urges his fellow believers, as well as people in general, to follow this path of ongoing creative evolution. It will not lead us away from God, he said, but more fully into the heart of the God who wills to share with us the process of creation.

However, if we take the path of evolution, if we see the future opening up before us, we still have to make a choice between whether we want to evolve on our own or in communion with others. With the emphasis on individualism in modern times it is a very strong temptation to go it alone. But individualism is ultimately an evolutionary dead end also. It is only by way of the path of communion, of joining cooperatively with others, that evolution advances. And we need not fear that joining with others is going to rob us of our individuality. In fact we are going to find our true and unique selfhood only by engaging along with others in "a great hope held in common."[12] There is a fundamental principle operative in evolution and in the nature of reality as such: *True union differentiates.* True union does not homogenize, does not reduce to uniformity. True union paradoxically lets the other be, and it lets the components of the more comprehensive unity achieve their freedom, their individuality, their mutual independence.[13]

Now how do we know this? We know this because if we look at the way evolution has worked in the past, we can see that it has moved from one level to the other only by passing recurrently through three phases: the phase of *divergence*, followed by *convergence*, followed by *emergence*. I cannot go into detail with each phase here, but let me exemplify the point by reference to living cells. As individual cells (single-celled forms of life) began to inhabit this planet, they spent—as we now know—a couple billion years simply spreading out over the face of the globe. This was the phase of divergence. But at a certain point in the past, a critical threshold was passed, and then the phase of convergence began to occur: The cells began to coagulate, first in looser associations, but then in tighter and more integrated forms of communion. That was the phase of convergence. Finally, at the point of very intense convergence, the emergence of something new, namely, multicelled, self-integrated organisms occurred.

So the pattern, once again, is: divergence, followed by convergence, followed by emergence. And this same pattern has repeated itself at various stages of matter's complexification. Now let us move to the latest dominant phase in evolution, when humans came onto the scene. Our species spent more than the first 100,000 years of its existence on this planet spreading out or diverging in tribal patterns of existence. Then about five to eight thousand years ago, in places like the Nile River basin and Mesopotamia, the individual human "cells" or tribes began to converge more tightly onto one another, first in the ancient city-states but more recently in the nation-states and even more recently in what Teilhard called planetization. If we look at what has been happening historically, politically, economically, and technologically, especially in communications technology, it would seem that we are going through a very tight type of convergence now. For all we know, we are just now passing the threshold from divergence to convergence—in an ambiguous and uncertain way. Now we have to imagine what life on Earth will be like, psychically speaking, Teilhard says, a million years from now, keeping in mind that a million years is not very long in evolutionary time. So we should not give up on ourselves. We are still very new to evolution. Is it possible that something new is now emerging through us without our being aware of it?[14]

Teilhard, in this respect, took seriously St. Paul's sense that the whole universe was straining for new creation, that the body of Christ was forming out of many members, and that it extended out to the whole universe. This Pauline vision was one that Teilhard wanted to transplant onto the evolutionary terrain of twentieth-century thought. What he saw happening now on our planet reminded him of what had occurred a long time ago in evolution when the primate brain became sufficiently complicated for the leap into "thought" to take place. The law of complexity-consciousness—the intensity of consciousness corresponds to the degree of organized physical complexity—permeates everything that Teilhard writes. And now we can see that a complexification process like that of the brain's evolution is occurring on a planetary scale: The Earth is weaving around itself something analogous to a brain. If the parallelism is instructive, why shouldn't we anticipate that something momentous is afoot on this Earth and, as I will show in a moment, possibly elsewhere in the universe as well. Isn't it possible that something new and unimaginably complex is still being created? And don't we have an obligation to participate in that adventure of creation?[15]

But now let us take these reflections even further and think about the possibility of intelligent life elsewhere in the universe. I think that if he were here today Teilhard would probably pay even more attention to this topic than in the few scattered allusions he did make to it. I believe that Teilhard's thought could be extended fruitfully into the age of SETI (The Search for Extraterrestrial Intelligence) in the following way.[16]

Let us start with what we know. We know that throughout the universe there has been a gradual increase in organized physical complexity, starting with preatomic matter, then moving on to atoms, molecules, and what Christian de Duve, the French biologist, has called "vital dust," referring to the carbon compounds that make up as much as 40 percent of interstellar dust. We know without a doubt that the complexification process has advanced at least this far throughout the cosmos. We also know that at least on Earth the process of complexifying matter has gone even further. Out of the vital dust have emerged cells, organisms, vertebrates, primates, and humans. And now the noosphere is beginning to take on an even more complex shape on a terrestrial scale. Who knows what else might emerge beyond that?

Now, according to Teilhard, we also know that in direct proportion to the increase in organized physical complexity, on our planet at least, there has been a corresponding increase in consciousness. So don't we have here a framework of inquiry, a heuristic perhaps, in terms of which we could make cosmic and theological sense of extraterrestrial intelligent life, that is, if we were ever do encounter it? Teilhard was experimenting only gingerly with such ideas during his life. But on the basis of his general understanding of evolution isn't it possible that if extraterrestrial intelligence turns out to be plentiful, then something like extraterrestrial noospheres are also in the process of being created? If this turns out to be the case, then these individual noospheres would become the cells, the atoms, the fundamental units of an unimaginable cosmic extension of consciousness. We don't yet know how this would be possible, since the noospheres would have to communicate with one another in some now unimaginable way if a newer phase of convergence is to occur. No doubt, these speculations will sound too wild for most people. But at least Teilhard provides an intelligible framework for locating such possibilities in the context of a purposeful universe.

Conclusion

Let me conclude these brief reflections by going back now to the question I asked earlier: Can cosmic purpose be an intelligible idea in an age of science? Human religious sensibilities were first shaped in terms of a prescientific, vertical hierarchy of being. Even to this day the spiritual lives of most of us, including scientists, have been molded by traditions that arose long before we had any sense of an evolving universe. How then can we map the vertical hierarchy of classic theology and philosophy onto the thirty-volume, horizontal unfolding of life, mind, and meaning out of lifeless and mindless matter?

Teilhard's answer to that question is not terribly complicated. First of all, think of God as "up ahead," and not just up above. In fact this is a very biblical way of thinking about God. The God of the Bible is the God who comes from the future, and urges or encourages the people of God to move toward the fulfillment that lies only in the future. The God of Abraham, the God of promise, draws the world toward unity from up ahead. God creates from out of the future. Second, think of the cosmic hierarchy not as a vertical but as an *emergent* hierarchy, one in which matter historically prepares the way for the appearance of life, life for mind, and mind for spirit. It is not so difficult, after all, as Teilhard himself proposed, to connect the great traditions—what I have been calling the Wisdom of the Ages—with the evolutionary world view. Just rearrange the religious furniture in your mind a little. Think of the world not so much as leaning on the past, and don't think of creation as something that takes place exclusively in the past, but think of the world as always "resting on the future," a future that for Teilhard is ultimately nothing other than God. God is the world's future, and it is as future that God is the world's ultimate support.[17] In this reconfiguration it is not inconceivable that the vine of religious meaning that traditionally wound itself around the vertical hierarchical latticework can now be transformatively rewound around the horizontal-evolutionary picture of a still unfinished creation.

CHAPTER TWO

Teilhard: Missionary to the Modern World

Thomas M. King, SJ

Teilhard had a close Jesuit friend, Rene d'Ouince, who knew him well over many years. Father d'Ouince spoke of Teilhard having "the blood of the great missionaries, a di Nobili, a Matteo Ricci setting out for unknown continents, eager to win the earth for Jesus Christ" (d'Q 340–41). Another Jesuit friend of Teilhard, Henri de Lubac, wrote at length of Teilhard's "apostolic soul" (dL, 10). Teilhard himself claimed he had a stronger call to the missions than did St. Francis Xavier (LT, 128). But the mission field that was calling him was not the Far East, it was the modern intellectual world. A world that had, in Teilhard's words, momentarily lost its God (AE, 278). For the first time since the coming of Christ, a civilization had developed new and powerful ways of understanding itself that did not include Christ. This Teilhard the missionary wanted to change.

But how does a missionary approach the modern world? In 1952 on the feast of St. Isaac Jogues and companions (Jesuit apostles to the Hurons and Iroquois martyred in the 1640s), Teilhard reflected in his journal about how the ideal of "conversion" that motivated Jogues and others was not the way to proceed: "The only thing that counts for me is not to propagate God, but to discover Him; from this conversion follows somewhat automatically" (J, Sep 26, 1952; see also July 13, 1951). People first needed "to discover" God, their God, and then conversion follows. On first going to China, he complained, "The missionaries here are pushing an artificial religion without a natural trunk" (UL, Gaudefroy, Aug 15, 1923). But the missionaries in China were not the only ones pushing a religion without a natural trunk. Church authorities in Rome were doing the same. For years Teilhard hoped to show Roman churchmen how the gospel should be preached to the world today. What would he show them?

Teilhard's great inspiration was St. Paul, the great missionary of the early church. St. Paul's mission began to the Jewish people. To them he tried to show how Christ was the climax of their history and was foretold in their sacred books. That was the natural trunk to which Paul appealed. But he did not preach only to the Jews; he preached to the Gentiles, and scripture shows us how. The Acts of the Apostles tells of his preaching to the Areopagites of Athens, the philosophers and cultural leaders of the ancient world. Paul told them of seeing in their city an altar inscribed, "To an unknown God." He continued, "What therefore you worship as unknown, this I proclaim to you" (Acts 17:23–28). Paul went on to quote an Athenian poet: "It is in him [God] we live and move and have our being." That is, he quotes *their* poet and refers to the unknown god whom *they already worshiped.* Paul spoke of this God as a presence in their life, one for whom they would search "and perhaps grope for him and find him." In all of this Paul is connecting his message with the natural trunk of their own culture and their own life. By their own life and history they had become aware of an unknown God, and Paul would show them how this was realized in the risen Christ.

Teilhard believed the scientists and naturalists of his time had come upon such a God and by their dedication practiced a "dark adoration" (LMF, 149, 96); through their work they felt an awesome and unnamed presence, and Teilhard believed that the Christian message would fit with what the scientific world was finding on its own. Teilhard would call their attention to the yet unnamed Presence they were "groping for" or feeling after and show this Presence to be Christ. Then conversion would follow almost automatically. When the "unknown God" was named, the dark adoration would become luminous. To know anyone personally the other must reveal one's self, that is, one must speak. In Christ the unknown God had attained a voice. But one must begin with a dark adoration that rises out of the experience of a culture or the direct experience of an individual.

First, rising from the experience of a culture: Teilhard would see the culture that has been developing in the West as largely shaped by science. He made many missionary approaches to this culture and wrote a masterpiece of missionary literature; he called it *The Phenomenon of Man*. This work can best be seen as an effort to help today's people with a scientific interest discover the God "they were groping for"; then it ends with several pages of assistance to show this God in the Christian faith. Conversion would be somewhat automatic.

The Phenomenon of Man is a lengthy account of what science has discovered about the nature and the history of the universe. He focuses on the buildup of ever more complex syntheses. At one point he gives a summary statement of what evolutionary biology has found:

> First the molecules of the carbon compounds with their thousands of atoms symmetrically grouped; next the cell which, within a very small volume, contains thousands of molecules linked in a complicated system; then the metazoa in which the cell is no more than an almost infinitesimal element; and later the manifold attempts made sporadically by the metazoa to enter into symbiosis and raise themselves to a higher biological condition. (P, 244)

Just as there is a soul of sorts uniting the elements in a cell, and a soul of sorts uniting the elements of a metazoa (ourselves), so today Teilhard would argue there is a Soul of sorts drawing humans together into a higher form. He would sometimes call this Soul a "World Soul." In the twentieth century he found many who spoke of this higher Soul as "humanity," and appeals to humanity had reshaped the politics of the globe. But, Teilhard warned, if the ideal is only "humanity," this could lead to Soviet society and the mechanization of individuals. So Teilhard argues for a personalizing center to humanity that he calls Omega; this Soul is uniting individuals to one another by their personal centers and uniting them to itself.

After 260 pages describing the evolution of life and the God/Soul implicit in the latter part of the process, Teilhard added an eight-page epilogue called "The Christian Phenomenon." Here he would have us look at Christianity with the eyes of a naturalist, that is, see it as a phenomenon connected with all that has been said. He makes three points concerning Christianity: First, he claims the kingdom of God—a central theme of the gospel—can be seen as "a prodigious biological operation" (P, 293). In this he connects the basic Christian claim with the biology he has considered. Secondly, though there are many ideologies in the world, he claims Christianity has gone beyond ideology in begetting life, for thousands of people daily are dedicating themselves to its ideals. Thirdly, he speaks of the vitality and growth of the Christian faith and asks, "Is not the Christian faith destined, is it not preparing, to save and even take the place of evolution?" Then he ends his book, "In the presence of such perfect coincidence, even if I were not a Christian, I think I would ask myself that question" (P, 297, 299). The missionary intent of the work has become clear.

In the body of *The Phenomenon of Man* Teilhard would help scientific-minded people discover God, their God. God would be the higher Soul that has been drawing the elements into ever more comprehensive unions and now is drawing us into union with one another and Itself. That is, he postulates an unknown God that he calls Omega, but a God intrinsic to the scientific process. Though it might not be identified by them as a God, it was, in the terms of St. Paul, that which they were feeling after and finding. The body of the book is to establish the base or trunk and the God implied, but a God they must discover on their own. When they had done so, he tells briefly of the Christian phenomenon, thus naming the unknown God as did St. Paul. He thinks conversion should more or less follow automatically.

Many of us know the story Teilhard tells of his childhood and how he was so fascinated by small pieces of iron that he referred to a "God of Iron." Finding that iron rusted, he turned his attention to the rocks and then to the Earth, the universe, the All. He tells how he felt divided between the appeal of the Christian God and the appeal of the Earth, the All. His faith was divided by the two contrary appeals. He opted for the Christian God and entered the Jesuits. As a young Jesuit he asked his novice director to let him forget about the rocks. But his novice director refused to do so. Teilhard was left holding two ends of string that were pulling him in opposite directions. Many years later this dualism ended when he saw that over the ages the rocks had undergone great changes in an evolutionary process that led to Jesus as Lord of evolution. His love of the rocks contained an implicit theology—had he not once referred to a "God of Iron"? He tells of practicing a devotion to this God in secrecy and silence. Was this not the dark adoration of which he later spoke? How could he set this aside as nothing? His novice director left him holding both elements: Christianity and the rocks, that is, his faith and its natural trunk.

Were the missionaries in China ignoring a "natural theology" the Chinese already had, ignoring an "unknown God" the Chinese people had "felt after and found"? Theirs was a God in whom, in the phrase of St. Paul, they lived and moved and had their being. Teilhard wanted the missionaries to help the people of China discover their God as *The Phenomenon of Man* might help Westerners discover the God they implicitly worshiped.

For many years Teilhard knew well an American sculptor, Lucile Swan; she was much engaged in her art work. In 1932 he wrote to her, "Your art is, I think, the sacred thread which, if followed, will lead you to the light which will be yours in the right time" (LS, 1). Lucile seemed to be "feeling after and finding" something in her work. Only by following that would she find her God—at the right time; this would be the trunk on which he would like to show her Christ as her God, and not as his. Lucile originally had little or no interest in religion, but soon took an interest in the religions of India. In 1949 she followed her guru to India and Teilhard wrote to her there, "India is a warm and tense atmosphere for any mystic, and I am sure you are going to feel closer to God (to *your* God) after this new experience of the East" (LS, 254). But believing that the Indian God she followed was "unconscious and impersonal" he pressed the point, asking her if that is what she wanted (LS, 271). Shortly before her death in 1965, she confessed to being a Christian; Teilhard had told her she would find her God "at the right time." It seems the trunk had to grow until she was ready.

But beyond her interest in sculpture, Lucile had an interest in Teilhard. She wrote in her journal, "I love you every minute of the day....I still love you so that it hurts—which is probably not the way you want me to love you" (LS, 18–19). Teilhard believed such love could also be a sacred thread and this he also tried to show her, and tried to show himself. During this friendship he wrote many articles telling how a chaste friendship can lead to God. In his feelings for her he too was following a sacred thread and believed it would lead both of them to God. Could either ignore the feelings they had for the other and still make one's "way to God *ex toto corde suo*" [with one's whole heart] (HM, 26)? Otherwise, one would be divided as he had been divided by his Christian faith and his "God of Iron." This missionary effort became known as the Third Way.

Teilhard had a good Jesuit friend, Auguste Valensin, who was a brilliant scholar with an abundance of publications. He had accepted the Catholic faith and then went about the academic and literary work that interested him. Was he finding some unknown God in his literary work and practicing a dark adoration of sorts, and at the same time saying the prescribed prayers to Jesus? Does that really work? Is such a one approaching God "ex toto corde suo"? There is a long spiritual tradition that would urge that we become indifferent to all created things, for no man can serve two masters. But Teilhard's novice director did not endorse that tradition, so he told Teilhard to maintain his interest in the rocks. Could the missionaries in China tell the Chinese to maintain their interest in Taoism, Confucianism, Buddhism, for it would be the "sacred thread" that would lead them to Christ "at the right time"? Yes, the Chinese would need the help of the missionaries to discover this, but they would discover it themselves. That way they could say to Jesus, "*My* Lord and *my* God," and love him with a full heart.

Teilhard was engaged by the rocks; he spoke of working in science as a devotee and saw many scientists bringing a sense of worship to their work. There are things that engage each of us. Did we ever consider this attraction to be a "sacred thread" that would lead us to God? It would be to a dark God that we might sense and yet be unable or unwilling to name. Teilhard would often speak of this God as the World Soul. The world itself has a loving Soul (it is Christ Jesus). This Soul shines through the matter of Earth. Teilhard would have it that it makes the Earth appear as flesh, flesh is matter animated with a soul—the fire has penetrated the Earth. It shines through the matter in thousands of fascinating ways. Each of us catches a different gleam, but we are to follow this gleam as a sacred thread. To change the image, we must develop the natural trunk upon which we can build our Christianity. For Teilhard would be a missionary to us, to me and you; children of a world that has temporarily lost its God. But when we find our God, it will not be grafted on the outside of the world or of ourselves. It will be rooted in the depths to which a sacred thread has led us.

St. Francis Xavier, the great Jesuit missionary of the sixteenth century, went among the fishermen of south India and there proclaimed the Christian gospel with great effect. The fishermen's culture was simple and they were in the process of adopting the higher culture that the Portuguese were bringing them wherein Jesus had a central place. His preaching had great effect. But then he went to Japan and encountered another high culture where there were no other Westerners. He became aware that he must proceed in a different way, he must immerse himself in the other culture and work from there (see La Couture, 135). This was the method later developed so well by later Jesuit missionaries, de Nobili in India and Matteo Ricci in China. It was the method of St. Paul in Athens. It was the method by which Teilhard would approach Western civilization. Recently some missionaries have come to have such respect for other cultures that they are unwilling to proclaim the Christian message. Some even have claimed they simply must help the people live their own culture and religion while bringing them more equitable social structures, and so forth. That would not be Teilhard. He would tell the people and tell you to follow your sacred thread, that gleam of the World Soul shining through your world. It will lead you along a difficult path, but follow it carefully to come to the unknown God that is yours, and you will find that God is Jesus, a Jesus that you can adore *ex toto corde tuo.*

Bibliography

Works by Teilhard

AE: *The Activation of Energy*, translated by Rene Hague. New York: Harcourt Brace Jovanovich, 1963.

HM: *The Heart of Matter*, translated by Rene Hague. New York: Harcourt Brace Jovanovich, 1978.

J, followed by a date: The unpublished journals of Teilhard. Available on a disc at the Woodstock Library, Georgetown University.

LMF: Letters *from My Friend Teilhard de Chardin*, translated by Mary Lukas. New York: Paulist Press, 1979.

LS: *Letters of Teilhard de Chardin and Lucile Swan*, edited by Thomas M. King, SJ, and Mary Wood Gilbert, introduction by Pierre Leroy, SJ. Scranton University Press, originally Georgetown University Press, 1993.

LT: *Letters from a Traveler*, translator not identified. New York: World Publishing, Meridian Books, 1969.

P: *The Phenomenon of Man*, translated by Bernard Wall. New York: Harper & Row, 1965.

UL followed by a name and date: An unpublished letter of Teilhard in the Georgetown University Library.

Works by Other Authors

d'Q: *L'homme de devant Dieu*, by Rene d'Quince. Paris: Eubier, 1964.

JMB: *The Jesuits: A Multibiography*, by Jean Lacouture, translated by Jeremy Leggatt. Washington: Counterpoint, 1993.

TE: *Teilhard Explained*, by Henri de Lubac, translated by Anthony Buono. New York: Paulist, 1968.

The scripture citations are from the Revised Standard Version.

CHAPTER THREE

Teilhard's Legacy in Science

Mark A. S. McMenamin

Introduction

The work of Marie Joseph Pierre Teilhard de Chardin, SJ, has greatly influenced the evolutionary sciences. This influence continues to grow, expanding both our understanding of the true scope of evolutionary processes and of the limitations of science as a way of knowing. Three areas can be identified where Teilhard's influence is most keenly felt. The first of these is in the study of convergent evolution, where Teilhard was considerably ahead of his scientific peers in understanding the phenomenon. The second is in consideration of monogenism in *Homo sapiens*, an area where Teilhard's uncritical acceptance of certain aspects of modernistic biology may have hindered our understanding of the origin of our species. The third is in consideration of, and rejection of, scientific positivism or scientism, where Teilhard made an early and very clear statement on the subject that still resonates today. In this chapter I will address each of these three areas in turn, and then conclude with some observations about Teilhard's overall impact on the sciences.

Convergent Evolution

The signal evolutionary debate of the twentieth century took place in Paris in 1949. Here, in a unique intellectual clash, Teilhard and his paleontologist friend and colleague George Gaylord Simpson tested one another at the *Colloquium sur paléontologie et transformisme* (McMenamin 1998). Teilhard used the term *transformism* as a synonym for the general theory of evolution (Lane 1996, p. 37). It now seems clear that Teilhard won the 1949 debate. In other words, the concept of a universe governed by chance and/or contingency (as posited by Simpson, Monod, Gould, Dawkins, and others) has fallen to the concept of a universe governed by purpose (Teilhard, Conway Morris, and others). Discussion of the key evidence that decides the argument follows.

Convergent evolution is the process by which similar morphological or behavioral traits are acquired by unrelated lineages of organisms. Examples of convergent evolution are rampant throughout the fossil record. Even George G. Simpson and his followers recognize that evolutionary convergences certainly do take place. Every few months we see publication of yet another example of convergence in *Science* or *Nature*.

It is important to recall that Teilhard was among the first to properly interpret the phenomenon of convergence, as perhaps best considered in his paleontological study of Chinese fossil mole rats (McMenamin 1998). These fossil mammals, small burrowing rodents from Cenozoic strata of China, are somewhat similar to modern mole rats but did not achieve the high degree of eusociality (the cooperative breeding in colonial insects such as bees and ants) as is seen in modern naked mole rats.

In his study of these fossil mammals, Teilhard showed that the main trunk of the Chinese mole rat family tree diverged into three separate branches that followed *separate but parallel* evolutionary trajectories. Similar traits then appeared in all three mole rat lineages. First, all the mole rats experienced an increase in body size. This is an example of Cope's Rule, the well-known tendency for maximum body size in successful animal lineages to increase over time. Second, each lineage developed continuous molar growth. This development is likely due to adaptation to a fossorial (burrowing) lifestyle. Third, all three lineages evolved fusion of the cervical vertebrae, a useful trait considering the stresses experienced in the neck and skull region by burrowing rodents.

Teilhard argued that this three-pronged example provided evidence for directionality in evolution. Simpsonians brushed aside his arguments by claiming that these adaptations were merely responses to similar environmental conditions by closely related animals. This complaint, however, has been dramatically undercut by documentation of an amazing number of instances of convergent evolution, particularly in unrelated lineages or in individual species that are not at all closely related (McMenamin 1998; Conway Morris 2003). In other words, Teilhard might have said yes, these are indeed all adaptations to common environmental conditions, but the multiple shared evolutionary trajectories also point to a tendency for the evolutionary process to follow predictable, or as Conway Morris (2003) puts it, inevitable paths. Extrapolating to the evolutionary processes of the entire biosphere, taken in aggregate, Teilhard argued that evolution was both directed and purposeful.

Aimée L. Gerbi's research showing simultaneous iterative evolution in two unrelated marine microbe lineages with different skeletal compositions (MacEachran 1996) strongly supports Teilhard's contention that directionality in evolution may be taken as a given. We should now elevate this concept to a principle of evolution. I propose calling this Teilhard's Rule: Generally predictable evolutionary trajectories are a characteristic of all lineages, and cases of evolutionary parallelism and convergence are the rule rather than the exception. Cope's Rule thus serves as a specific case of the more general Teilhard's Rule.

The applicability of Teilhard's Rule has been further demonstrated by recent reports of convergences between eusocial insects and eusocial mammals (McMenamin 1998; Conway Morris 2003; references therein). Simon Conway Morris (2003) catalogued more astonishing examples of convergence, including an eye with lens on a mysid shrimp (convergent on vertebrate and molluskan eyes, themselves convergent) and the convergence between the predatory forelimbs of the preying mantis and the otherwise unrelated neuropteran insect *Mantispa*. The mysid shrimp thus has the odd characteristic of bearing both arthropod compound eyes and camera eyes. Given enough arthropod lineages and evolutionary time, Teilhard's Rule predicts that other lineages of arthropods would eventually develop camera eyes. In fact, it may be possible to retrodict this prediction, in other words, make predictions about ancient life forms. An inventory needs to be made of extinct arthropods (such as *Anomalocaris*; Cambrian, 535 million years ago) and arthropod-like animals (such as *Tullimonstrum*; Pennsylvanian Period, 300 million years ago) to determine if these and other such organisms added camera eyes to an originally compound set.

Alberto G. Sáez and Encarnación Lozano (2005) describe discovery of numerous cryptic species, species so similar in morphology that measurement of genetic variation is required to tell them apart. To the well-known example of convergence between placental saber-toothed cats (*Smilodon* and saber-tooths such as *Hoplophoneus*) and a saber-toothed South American marsupial (*Thylacosmilus*) must now be added evidence for the independent origins of middle ear bones in both monotremes and therian (marsupial and placental) mammals (Martin and Luo 2005; Rich et al. 2005). As if this were not enough, we can add examples of the independent evolution of tribosphenid teeth in monotremes and therians. To the list of flying and gliding vertebrates must be added a new order of Jurassic gliding mammals, typified by the new genus *Volaticotherium*. Dale Russell's striking sculpture (by taxidermist Ron Sequin) of a hypothetical hominin-like descendant of the dinosaur *Troödon* has generated considerable comment for decades, and has been recently nicknamed "Smartasaurus." Russell based his thought experiment on measurable increases in dinosaurian EQ (Encephalization Quotient) over the course of the Mesozoic. The recent discovery of opposable fingers in the maniraptoran dinosaur *Bambiraptor* adds considerable credence to Russell's speculations. Teilhard's Rule thus seems to be a law of nature. But what exactly do we mean by a law of nature? We will consider this question further.

The Monogenism Problem

Teilhard's work was heavily focused on the search for evidence for human evolution. This was a primary motivation for his project to map the Cenozoic strata of China and surrounding regions, and this research program met with success with the discovery of Peking Man at Chou-Kou-Tien (Aczel 2007). In the course of this research Teilhard adopted an evolutionistic approach to human evolution and origins. This orientation caused him to reject monogenism out of hand, as he could see no way that the ancestral human population size could ever have been as small as a single couple, a single man and a single woman. This perspective, incidentally, sets Teilhard against more recent and rather convincing critics of an obsolete evolutionistic approach, that is, one that restricts discussion to consideration of incremental, gradual change governed by natural selection.

Could our species be traced back to a single couple? Ayala (1995) estimated that the original population of *Homo sapiens* could never have numbered fewer than about ten thousand individuals, but his estimate is beholden to assumptions of gradualistic evolutionary change. The fact remains that the generative factors associated with the origin of new species are still poorly understood, rendering the assumptions on which Ayala (1995) bases his calculations rather suspect. For example, hybrids of the butterfly species *Lycaeides melissa* and *L. ida* give rise to individuals that are reproductively isolated from either parent species but which can breed with one another (Gompert et al. 2006). This represents a case of convergent evolution taken to an almost absurd extreme, and the third (and yet unnamed) species created in this fashion has an unusual mosaic genome that would confound gradualistic, neo-Darwinisitic estimates of population size at the time of species emergence. The implications of this for the possibility of human monogenism can be considered as follows. Imagine that hominin species A mates with hominin species B to form a male of new species C. Hominin species A again mates with hominin species B, to form a female of new species C. Male C is somehow introduced to female C, and this would of course be the origin of the first human pair-bond. Does this sound far-fetched? Then consider this recent evidence concerning the human speciation event (Patterson, N., et al., 2006, "Genetic evidence for complex speciation of humans and chimpanzees". *Nature* [advance online publication] DOI: 10.1038/nature04789 and http://www.broad.mit.edu/cgi-bin /news/display_news. cgi?id=1001 and http://www.hhmi.org/news /lahn20061006.html):

> The results show that the two species [chimps and humans] split no more than 6.3 million years ago and probably less than 5.4 million years ago. Moreover, the speciation process was unusual—possibly involving an initial split followed by later hybridization before a final separation. "The study gave unexpected results about how we separated from our closest relatives, the chim-panzees. We found that the population structure that existed around the time of human-chimpanzee speciation was unlike any modern ape population. Something very unusual happened at the time of speciation," said David Reich, the senior author of the *Nature* paper, and an asso-ciate member of the Broad Institute and assistant profes-sor at Harvard Medical School's Department of Genetics.

Thus it is entirely possible that humanity could be traced back to a very small number of individuals, perhaps initially two with plausibly a few others sired in an unusual speciation event resulting from an intimate encounter between two distinct hominin populations not belonging to the same species. Epigenetic effects, involving dynamical patterning modules or other factors, are now being invoked to explain rapid evolutionary change. Evolutionary biologist Stuart Newman cautions us about a worrisome corollary, namely, the possibility that experimentation with the human genomic and other developmental factors could have abrupt and profoundly troubling results. In other words, human monogenism implies that attempts to engage in "human genetic enhancement" could lead to an unforeseen homonin speciation event. This frightening prospect has led Francis Fukuyama to call consideration of any such attempt "the world's most dangerous idea."

The Challenge to Positivism

One of Teilhard's first published papers is perhaps the most important and least appreciated research article of the twentieth century (Teilhard 1909). The article appeared in the Jesuit journal *Études*. Some Teilhard researchers have dismissed this paper as mere juvenilia, and not representative of Teilhard's mature thought. A realization of the importance of this paper, however, is slowly dawning (Graef 1962; King 2005). In this early paper Teilhard rightly chastises the scientific community for failing to seriously ponder the implications of the healings at the Lourdes grotto in France. Mixing his analysis with some brusque commentary, Teilhard picks apart objections to scientific recognition of the Lourdes phenomenon, leaving the arguments against in utter shambles. Regarding doctors who had visited and studied Lourdes, Teilhard writes:

> *Quelle conclusion définitive, acceptée, s'en dégage pour la science? aucune. Ce serait logique pourtant: il s'agit de choses observables, qu'on peut aller voir à coup sûr, et étudier aussi à l'aise qu'une éclipse de soleil. Mais la science officielle se tait; elle feint d'ignorer, ou recule devant*

l'explication, boudant des phénomènes qui la gênent, infidèle à son caractère d'impartialité et de respect absolu du fait.

[What definitive and accepted conclusion have they gained for science? Nothing. It however would be logical—these are things that can be observed and studied with the relative ease of observing a solar eclipse. But Official Science falls silent, and pretends to ignore or to hesitate before explaining. Science as a whole is quite cool towards these phenomena, an attitude untrue to Science's presumed character of impartiality and her absolute respect for facts. (Translation by Mark A. S. McMenamin)]

The difficulty of comprehending the scientific implications of any kind of miracle is daunting to say the least. What "law of nature" is *not* violated by such events? Teilhard actually does try to identify the laws not violated at Lourdes. But as Teilhard so shrewdly pointed out in his 1909 paper, denial of the existence of such events is not consonant with honest and impartial (not to mention empirical) scientific investigation.

Teilhard's 1909 paper thus encourages us to avoid the trap of a self-deluding *scientism*. The tendency to scientism comes into play when naturalistic explanations are attributed to events *after* the search for a natural explanation has been exhausted. The search for natural explanation is a required first step, of course, but going beyond reasonable or even strenuous efforts in this regard is an instance of the kind of Western scientific extrapolationism that was so roundly criticized by Vladimir Vernadsky (Vernadsky 1998). Vernadsky might even have picked up this concept from Teilhard himself, who wrote that "nothing is more illusory than extrapolation."

The challenge to scientific positivism may be posed in the following fashion, as a thought experiment intended to get us thinking in ways that those of us who work in science might not ordinarily be inclined to think. The *gedanken* is as follows: What if the witnesses of the best-known post-1909 alleged Marian apparitions (Fatima, 1917; Zeitoun, 1968–71) were actually witnessing something that was authentic, in the sense of an event that was really happening? The Wikipedia entries for these two apparitions are unevenly matched, with the Fatima article being favorably disposed to accept the apparition and the current Zeitoun article appearing as biased against the apparition. The so-called Miracle of the Sun in 1917 in Fatima was witnessed by tens of thousands of people, and Marian apparitions at Zeitoun were also seen by at least that many, and perhaps many more in a predominately Islamic country.

Eighty years after Teilhard's landmark paper on Lourdes, Michael A. Persinger and John S. Deer (Persinger and Deer 1989) argued that the Zeitoun apparitions were the result of tectonic strain on a fault system more than one hundred kilometers from Zeitoun. This study, in addition to being comically unreasonable from a geological perspective, suffers from such a swarm of methodological problems that Persinger's work has been subjected to severe methodological criticism (Rutkowski 1984). The Persinger and Deer (1989) study can be viewed as scientism at its worst, and something that should give practicing scientists cause for, well, soul-searching. For example, consider a breathtakingly inadequate treatment of apparition evidence by one of science's most famous modern practitioners—Carl Sagan. Sagan's flawed discussion of Marian apparitions (Sagan 1996) seems quite opposed to any serious attempt to actually understand the phenomenon. See Carroll (1986) for an arguably even worse attempt to explain apparitions away as a psychological phenomenon (pareidolia). Carroll, unlike Sagan, at least admits the inexplicable nature of the phenomenon (Carroll 1986, p. 216: "it seems wisest to say that in all these cases we simply do not know what produced these visual events"). Fortunately, willingness to consider at least the possibility that the apparitions are authentic events has gained recent widespread support among both skeptics (for example, Harris 1999) and believers (for example, McMenamin 2006). This of course does not require that every alleged apparition is authentic; all caveats applied by the church to the discernment of such things would certainly apply. We can say that Fatima and Zeitoun at least seem to have the approval of local church authorities, and furthermore Fatima has approval from the Roman Catholic Church.

How is one accustomed to interpreting the world through the lens of naturalistic science to interpret the scientific implications of such things? I think that at a minimum, after considering Fatima and Zeitoun, we as scientists must humbly admit that naturalistic, scientistic, and/or materialistic views of the world are woefully incomplete.

Conclusions

Writing in *Geobiologia*, a journal he cofounded, Teilhard (1943) argued:

Besides the incontestable advantages of [Simpson's mechanistic] attitude (which obliges the biologist to analyze and to take apart the mechanisms of morphogenesis), it has...an evident weakness. In its obstinate refusal to look at the indisputable psychic ascent (invention) that globally accompanies the expansion and the arrangement of the biosphere, it deprives the evolutionary process of all direction and all significance as a whole, bringing about the particularly serious result of leaving the human phenomenon unexplained, and scientifically not understandable.

Teilhard was surely correct to say this. Recent arguments from critiques of convergent evolution, monogenism, and positivism *all* add strength to this conclusion. Is such a perspective tenable in terms of secularistic science? Perhaps it might be better to say that secularistic science risks its own validity as an intellectually valid endeavor if it folds its arms and huffily turns its back on this perspective.

St. Albert the Great, doctor of the church, laid out the scope of the natural sciences as follows: "In studying nature we have not to inquire how God the Creator may, as He freely wills, use His creatures to work miracles and thereby show forth His power: we have rather to inquire what Nature with its immanent causes can naturally bring to pass" (*De Coelo et Mundo*, I, tr. iv, x). Teilhard (1966, p. 101) appears to second this concept when he speaks of "a certain physical 'immanence' (forgive the philosophical term) in life." St. Albert the Great's specification of the terms of scientific research has served us well for centuries, but it does not rule out the possibility that study of the immanent causes of Nature might on occasion bring us face to face with the transcendent. As St. Augustine put it, "Miracles do not happen in contradiction to nature, but only in contradiction to what is known to us of nature." This I believe is the ultimate scientific legacy of Teilhard's work. Teilhard was well ahead of his time in attempts to understand the significance of convergent evolution. He understood the difficulties that convergence posed for a chance/contingency perspective of evolutionary change. Teilhard also grasped the support that convergent evolution provided to the view that laws of evolution (such as Teilhard's Rule) exist that render particular evolutionary pathways more or less inevitable. Unfortunately, Teilhard's thinking fell prey to a gradualistic evolutionism that led him to reject monogenism out of hand. The language he uses in *The Vision of the Past* (p. 157) betrays this bias when he predicts that monogenism will "*gradually* assume a form fully conforming to our scientific requirements [italics added]." This attitude is linked to Teilhard's heterodox thinking about original sin and his eventual exile from France to China. In spite of these problems, Teilhard can and has influenced our approach to science (Heller 1995), given us a keen sense of its strengths and limitations, and imbued us with a sense of the Ignatian imperative to find God in all things.

References

Aczel, A. 2007. *The Jesuit and the Skull: Teilhard de Chardin, Evolution, and the Search for Peking Man.* Riverhead Hardcover, New York.

Carroll, M. P. 1986. *The Cult of the Virgin Mary.* Princeton University Press, Princeton.

Conway Morris, S. 2003. *Inevitable Humans in a Lonely Universe.* Cambridge University Press, Cambridge.

Deer, J. S., and M. A. Persinger. 1989. Geophysical variables and behavior: LIV. Zeitoun (Egypt) apparitions of the Virgin Mary as tectonic strain-induced luminosities. *Perceptual and Motor Skills* 68:123–28.

Gompert, Z., J. A. Fordyce, M. L. Forister, A. M. Shapiro, and C. C. Nice. 2006. "Homoploid hybrid speciation in an extreme habitat." *Science* 314:1923–25.

Graef, H. 1962. *Mystics of Our Times.* Burns and Oates, London.

Harris, R. 1999. *Lourdes: Body and Spirit in the Secular Age.* Viking, New York.

Heller, M. 1995. "Teilhard's vision of the world and modern cosmology." *Zygon* 30:11–23.

King, T. M., SJ. 2005. "Dieu et l'Avenir de l'Humanité." Pp. 38–42 in *La Philosophie of* [sic] *Teilhard dans la Construction de l'Avenir de l'Humanité,* Fordham University, New York.

Lane, D. H. 1996. *The Phenomenon of Teilhard: Prophet for a New Age.* Mercer University Press, Macon, Georgia.

Martin, T., and Z.-X. Luo. 2005. "Homoplasy in the mammalian ear." *Science* 307(5711):861–62.

MacEachran, A. L. 1996. *Iterative Evolution sans Associated Extinction: The Agglutinated and Calcareous Paleozoic Foraminifera.* Unpublished Honors Thesis, Mount Holyoke College, South Hadley, Massachusetts.

McMenamin, M. 2006. "Our Lady of Guadalupe and Eucharistic Adoration." *Numismatics International Bulletin* 41(5):91–97.

McMenamin, M. A. S. 2003. "Origin and early evolution of predators: The ecotone model and early evidence for macropredation." Pp. 379–400 in P. H. Kelley, M. Kowalewski, and T. A. Hansen, eds., *Predator-Prey Interactions in the Fossil Record.* Kluwer Academic/Plenum Publishers, New York.

McMenamin, M. A. S. 2001. *The Evolution of the Noösphere.* American Teilhard Association for the Future of Man Teilhard Studies 42, New York. ISBN 0890120854.

McMenamin, M. A. S. 1998. *The Garden of Ediacara: Discovering the First Complex Life.* Columbia University Press, New York.

Rich, T. H., J. A. Hopson, A. M. Musser, T. F. Flannery, and P. Vickers-Rich. 2005. "Independent origins of middle ear bones in monotremes and therians." *Science* 307 (5711):910–14.

Rutkowski, C. A. 1984. "Geophysical variables and human behavior: XVI. Some criticisms." *Perceptual and Motor Skills* 58:840–42.

Sáez, A., and E. Lozano. 2005. "Body doubles." *Nature* 433:111.

Sagan, C. 1996. *The Demon-Haunted World.* Ballantine Books, New York.

Teilhard de Chardin, M. J. P., SJ. 1909. "Les miracles de Lourdes et les enquêtes canoniques." *Études* 118:161–83.

Teilhard de Chardin, M. J. P., SJ. 1943. "Quantitative zoology according to Dr. G. G. Simpson." *Geobiologia* 1:139–41.

Teilhard de Chardin, M. J. P., SJ. 1966. *The Vision of the Past.* Collins, St. James's Place, London.

Vernadsky, V. I. 1998. *The Biosphere.* Copernicus, New York.

CHAPTER FOUR

Teilhard and the World Soul

Ewert Cousins

Introduction

Teilhard's theology is emphatically focused on the cosmic Christ. In fact, it was Teilhard who reawakened an awareness in modern times of the ancient doctrine of the Cosmic Christ. However, in this paper I would like to focus on a different aspect of Teilhard's theology that he explored in his early writings and that deserves to be brought to light in our times, namely, his exploration of the ancient doctrine of the World Soul.

The World Soul

The World Soul is one of the three divine principles in the Platonic-Neoplatonic tradition. It first appeared in the fourth century BCE in the dialogue of Plato entitled *Timaeus*. It became a classical element in the Platonic tradition, featuring in the synthesis of Plotinus in the third century CE, in the Platonists of Chartres in the twelfth century, and again in Renaissance Platonism. Since the Neoplatonic tradition was assimilated by Christianity, Judaism, and Islam, it was drawn into these traditions. It stands in sharp contrast to the mechanism of Enlightenment science, and it has striking affinities with twenty-first-century science and with the philosophy of organism of Whitehead, as well as with the Gaia hypothesis proposed by ecologists. The following quotation from the *Enneads* of Plotinus gives the essence of the doctrine of the World Soul in such a way that it resonates with the holistic, earth-centered spirituality of the primal peoples:

> Now to understand how life is imparted to the universe and to each individual, the soul must rise to the contemplation of The Soul, the soul of the world. The individual soul, though different from The Soul, is itself no slight thing. Yet it must become worthy of this contemplation: freed of the errors and seductions to which other souls are subject, it must be quiet. Let us assume that quiet too is the body that wraps it round—the quiet earth, quiet the air and the sea, quiet the high heavens. Then picture the soul flowing into this tranquil mass from all sides, streaming into it, spreading through it until it is luminous. As the rays of the sun lighten and gild the blackest cloud, so The Soul by entering the body of the universe gives it life and immortality; the abject it lifts up. The universe, moved eternally by an intelligent Soul, becomes blessed and alive. The Soul's presence gives value to a universe that before was no more than an inert corpse, water and earth...[1]

In the complete Neoplatonic worldview, the World Soul emanates from a transcendent principle called the Intelligence, from which it receives the intelligible forms that it imparts to the material world; and the Intelligence itself emanates from the ultimate transcendent principle, the One. It is easy to see structurally how, with the impetus to transcendence, the World Soul could become fragmented off from the other principles and recede into the background. This is precisely what happened in the history of Christianity where the World Soul was correlated with the Holy Spirit. This left the material world as an autonomous realm that could easily become the world machine of Enlightenment science, devoid of divine presence and of its own organic vitality.

From a psychological viewpoint, Christians have experienced the Spirit primarily in the human sphere in their moral and spiritual life, and not the geosphere and biosphere. The early Christians felt the power of the Spirit transforming their souls, imparting charisms and uniting the community in a bond of love. The newness of life in the Spirit was so profound and overwhelming that cosmic dimensions received little stress. As the church spread, the Christian experience of spiritual transformation encountered the Greek cosmic sense. The Greek fathers gave expression to the cosmic dimensions largely through their development of the doctrine of the Trinity and its relation to creation. The cosmic dimension was also developed in Western medieval theology, especially among the Platonists of Chartres and the Franciscans, but by the late Middle Ages certain juridical, abstract, and individual tendencies in Western theology, tending to obscure the cosmic sense, gained ascendancy. At the Reformation, of course, the burning issue was the justification of the Christian, and debate focused on whether the Spirit worked within or outside the rites and juridical structures of the Roman Church. Theologians saw Christ in his role of redeemer from sin, not in relation to creation and the cosmic process. This period also saw the beginning of modern science with its own methods of investigating the physical universe. While the religious controversy raged on the spiritual level, cosmic concern passed to the scientists, who had to struggle with the religious establishment in order to vindicate the autonomy of their method. There emerged a scientific interest in the cosmos that became increasingly secularized and divorced from religion. The result of this dichotomy was that Teilhard's attempts to present a vision that encompassed both the physical sciences and the religious sphere were looked upon with suspicion by both camps.

In the history of theology, the doctrine of the cosmic Spirit is grounded in the doctrine of creation. Although there is a tendency in theology to relate creation to the Father, redemption to the Son, and sanctification to the Holy Spirit, there is another tradition, quite ancient, that sees the creation of the universe grounded in the processions of the persons in the Trinity. In this latter tradition, the three persons of the Trinity have a dynamic role in the creation of the universe. Creation begins with the Father, advances through the Son, and is completed through the Spirit. Gregory of Nyssa gives a concise formulation:

> ...the fountain of power is the Father, and the power of the Father is the Son, and the spirit of that power is the Holy Spirit; and Creation entirely, in all its visible and spiritual extent, is the finished work of that Divine power...we should be justified in calling all that Nature which came into existence by creation a movement of Will, an impulse of Design, a transmission of Power, beginning from the Father, advancing through the Son, and completed in the Holy Spirit.[2]

Gregory was writing against a group that maintained that the Spirit had no part in creation. In a passage that contains a humorous overtone, he writes:

> For if heaven, and the earth, and all created things were really made through the Son and from the Father, but apart from the Spirit, what was the Holy Spirit doing at the time when the Father was at work with the Son upon the Creation? Was He employed upon some other works, and was this the reason that He had no hand in the building of the Universe?[3]

Having been active in creation, the Spirit does not withdraw from the world, but acts as a dynamic presence throughout the universe. Gregory Nazianzen sees the Spirit as a universal presence in the world: "For He is the maker of all these, filling the world in His essence, containing all things, filling the world in His essence, yet incapable of being comprehended in His power by the world."[4] Although he is a universal presence and power in the world, he is also present in baptized Christians in a new way, but similar in its creative power; for he is "the Creator-Spirit who by Baptism and by resurrection creates anew; the Spirit that knows all things, that teaches, that blows where and to what extent He wishes."[5] Thus the Greek theologians can compare and yet contrast the two creations: the creation from nonbeing and the new creation into the divine life. They have no difficulty in linking the Spirit to both, without at the same time reducing the level of sanctification to that of the original creation. Behind this vision is a metaphysics of levels of perfection in the created universe, which allows the theologians to see the activity of the Spirit on each level proportioned to the perfection of that level.

While the concept of multileveled activity allowed Christian theologians to see the Spirit operating throughout the universe, it also enabled them to tap the resources of Greek philosophy and integrate these into their Christian worldview. Hence they were able to attribute to the Holy Spirit the functions that Platonism and Neoplatonism had assigned to the *anima mundi*, or World Soul, a concept with deep roots in the history of religion and philosophy.[6] The World Soul idea emerges out of a primitive numinous awareness of the presence of the divine in nature, which in its early forms expressed itself in animism and polytheism, with cults of nature gods. The cosmic religious sense merged with the philosophical sense of the One in the thought of the pre-Socratic Greek cosmologists.

Aware of the unity of the cosmos, they sought to explore its rational structures. The Platonists called the unifying principle of the cosmos the World Soul, but balanced its immanent functions by its emanation from the transcendent realm. For the Neoplatonists, the World Soul was the third hypostasis, emanating from Intelligence, which in turn, emanates from the One. Emanating from Intelligence, the World Soul goes out to form and order the material world and to act as an immanent principle of life and growth. Christian theologians were strongly influenced by these philosophical traditions.

It was in the context of Platonic and Neoplatonic thought that Christian theologians developed their doctrine of trinitarian processions and the dynamic activity of the Trinity in the cosmic emanation and return. Against Neoplatonic subordinationism, Christian theologians affirmed the consubstantiality of the Son and Spirit with the Father. At the same time, they drew heavily from elements in the philosophical traditions. Writing on the doctrine of the World Soul, Tullio Gregory observes that "in general all the Greek theologians not only found in the first two hypostases of the Neoplatonic triad the representation of the Father and the Son, but they also completed the correlation by attributing to the Holy Spirit the functions of the *anima mundi*....."[7] To link the World Soul with the Holy Spirit has significant theological results. It makes a bold affirmation of immanence and transcendence, bringing together the highest reality, a person of the Trinity, with the lowest level of matter. It thus forestalls any explicit or implicit dualism, which would conceive of the material world as basically alien or hostile to God. It also makes an emphatic affirmation of the unity of the cosmic process, for although the Spirit acts on each level in a way proportioned to that level, he acts in the same generic way throughout the universe—bringing order and form to creation and acting as a source of life and growth, leading creation to its fulfillment.

While the Greek theologians tended to relate the Holy Spirit to the World Soul, the Latins on the contrary hesitated to do so, although there were a few exceptions. Because of the strong Platonic influence in the twelfth-century school of Chartres, for example, it is not surprising to find William of Conches writing of the World Soul.[8] In a common medieval tradition flowing through Boethius, Pseudo-Dionysius, and John Scotus Erigena, William sees that the force energizing the cosmos is that of love.[9] He then identifies this cosmic love with the World Soul of Plato and links this with the Holy Spirit:

The World Soul is the natural energy [vigor] by which some things merely move, others grow, others sense, others think. But we ask: What is that energy? Now as it seems to me, the natural energy is the Holy Spirit, that is the divine and benign harmony, which is that by which all things have being, move, grow, sense, live, think.[10]

William was not alone in linking the World Soul with the Spirit; this was common to a whole current of twelfth-century theology.[11] However, the movement did not gain momentum because of the criticism of William of St. Thierry and the condemnation of Abelard.[12] Also with the recovery of the text of Aristotle in the twelfth and thirteenth centuries there entered into the Western intellectual tradition an understanding of nature as autonomous, not requiring for its full functioning a transcendent principle like the World Soul.

Teilhard and the World Soul

This background provides a perspective for some of Teilhard's own comments on the World Soul. In 1918 he wrote an essay entitled "The Soul of the World," printed in the volume *Writings in Time of War*.[13] Beneath the surface of our experience, he says, we can detect a soul of the world: "Whichever road we follow, we cannot withdraw from the superficial plane of day to day relationships without finding *immediately behind us, as if it were an extension of ourselves, a soul of the world*."[14] Throughout history, the true poets have felt its presence, "in the solitude of the deserts, in nature's fruitful breath, in the fathomless swell of the human heart."[15] The World Soul has "provided fuel for human enthusiasm and passion in their most intense forms."[16] Although its influence has been felt throughout history, it seems to be emerging from greater force and clarity:

Even so, with the passage of time, its radiating influence seems to become progressively more distinctly recog-

nizable, and more and more indispensable for our intellectual and emotional satisfaction. It will not be long
before no structure of truth or goodness can be built up
without a central position being reserved for that soul,
for its influence and its universal mediation.[17]

The explorations of science into the energies of matter and
the heightening of social awareness have directed attention to
the Soul of the World, which "is gradually emerging all around
us, as an absorbing and inevitable Reality."[18] In his religious perspective, Teilhard sees an intimate connection between the World
Soul and Christ:

Through the soul of the world, and through the soul
alone the Word, becoming incarnate in the universe, has
been able to establish a vital, immediate, relationship
with each one of the animate elements that make up the
cosmos.

Through the soul, accordingly, and for all time, the
humano-divine influence of Christ encompasses us,
penetrates us, identifies itself with all the forces of our
growth as individuals and as a social whole.[19]

In this essay Teilhard was expressing the same type of
awareness and struggling with the same problems that have surrounded the questions of the World Soul in the history of philosophy and theology. Teilhard's World Soul combines the numinous
awareness of the divine in the universe with the philosophical
sense of unity. Furthermore, the World Soul is a vital, energizing
force in the cosmos. Although he points out the relation between
the World Soul and Christ, he does not associate the World Soul
with the Spirit. Teilhard's later writings do not develop this out-
line of his concept of the World Soul. In his later writings he does
not develop this concept as a major theme, but associates the
related themes more and more with the cosmic Christ.

Nevertheless, this early essay provides a link in a chain of evidence giving support to the significance of a latent theology of the cosmic Spirit in Teilhard's thought.

We can now draw into focus his specific emphasis and evaluate his contributions. The theology of creation, stemming from the Greek fathers and moving through Western medieval theology, sees creation proceeding from the Father through the Son and completed in the Holy Spirit. Teilhard does not focus on the origin of things and develop what could be called a theology of the Father as ultimate source. Nor does he focus on the created world as reflecting back to its divine exemplar and develop a theology of the Son as archetype of creation as Bonaventure does. Rather, he focuses on the movement of the cosmos toward its end. This is precisely the point of view of the Spirit; for in the theology of appropriation, finality is appropriated to the Spirit. Thus Teilhard's emphasis coincides with the theology of the Spirit, and specifically with the theology of the cosmic Spirit; for he studies fulfillment and finality not within the trinitarian life, but within the cosmos itself.

What Teilhard sees as the immanent love energy of the cosmos, the theological tradition saw as the action of the transcendent Spirit, who is the love of the Father and the Son. Both Teilhard and the theological tradition affirm absolute immanence and transcendence. Although the transcendent is immanent in all levels of the cosmos—even in a speck of dust or an atom—the transcendent is not present in all levels in the same way, but according to the perfection of the level. The Spirit works in the plant kingdom as the ultimate source of vital energy, but is not present in his full personal reality because the plants are not persons and do not have the power to receive or give a personal response. They are, in the classical phrase, only vestiges of the Trinity. However, human beings can respond in a personal way since they are images of the Trinity. Finally, on the level of grace, the Spirit is present to human beings in a most personal way, transforming them into the likeness of the Trinity. This approach is based on two principles: (1) the immanence of the transcendent divinity in all levels of the universe; (2) varying degrees of divine presence based on the relative perfection of creatures.

These two principles were the foundation of the cosmic theology of the Greek fathers and of the Western medieval theologians, and they also form the basic structure of Teilhard's vision. For Teilhard sees the immediate action of Christ-Omega throughout the cosmos and at the same time maintains the graded presence and action of Omega in the geosphere, biosphere, and sphere of human consciousness.

While Teilhard shares many elements with the classical theological tradition, he also makes an original contribution that is the result of his personal genius and his being a person of the twentieth century. In 1918 Teilhard wrote that "the soul of the world is gradually emerging all around us, as an absorbing and inevitable Reality."[20] Through advances in scientific knowledge, we have broken out of our static universe and enlarged our horizons. We no longer see ourselves as actors on a cosmic stage or as spectators of a cosmic drama. We are now part of the process and the process is part of us. We are turned toward an open future that awakens hope and anxiety. In an age in which evolution has become conscious of itself, we know that we have the possibility and the awesome responsibility of shaping the future structure of our universe. We have already extended our consciousness in all directions: into the energy of the subatomic world, by encircling the Earth with a web of electronic communication, by establishing a foothold in outer space. All this is part of what Teilhard calls the process of complexification and planetization, leading to a new form of integral consciousness in which the highest powers of humanity will be integrated with the most elemental physical energy and channeled toward Omega. It is this modern experience that Teilhard has in mind when he speaks of the World Soul emerging. And it is this modern experience—so keenly perceived and so brilliantly expressed by Teilhard—that is the new dimension he adds to the tradition of the cosmic Spirit. The divine energy that flows from the

Father through the Son to reach its creative completion in the Spirit is felt by the modern person in an extraordinary way. For the modern person feels there is nothing static in the universe since all is caught up in the process and the process is becoming conscious of itself. In the light of the emerging modern experience, then, we can see the divine energy acting in the universe in a way even more striking than classical theology had conceived.

The theology of the Holy Spirit is a key to Teilhard's view of cosmic evolution. It is true that Teilhard constantly points to Christ the Omega, who is the goal and the motive force in evolution; but as a matter of fact, it is the process itself that he emphasizes. It is the movement, the dynamism, the openness to the development that one senses in Teilhard's writings. For Teilhard sees the goal as inaugurating the process and as being achieved through the process. He makes us aware that we are not frozen in a static slot in a static world; rather, we are moving in a dynamic process that sweeps along every particle of the universe.

In Teilhardian vocabulary the central word is *genesis*; for he sees all levels of the universe caught up in a genesis, or process of becoming. It is this process of genesis that he describes in detail in *The Phenomenon of Man*.[21] It has been said that the modern person has discovered history and process. Using Teilhardian terminology, we can say that the nineteenth century discovered genesis in the sphere of consciousness, through Hegelian philosophy, and in the development of the tools of critical historical research. Darwin extended the awareness of genesis to the biosphere through his theory of the evolution of species. Twentieth-century physics and chemistry have explored the theoretical possibility of genesis in the geosphere—in the inorganic and subatomic world. What Teilhard has done is to integrate all these levels of genesis into an organic process that he calls cosmogenesis and that reaches its fulfillment on the religious level in Christogenesis.

On the one hand, Teilhard brings the modern experience into the theology of the cosmic Spirit; on the other, his thought, seen in the context of the history of the theology of the Spirit, leads to the solution of certain theological problems at the same time that it raises others. For example, the presence of the Spirit in the universe overcomes any Gnostic or Manichean dualism; for there is no realm of the universe where the Spirit is not present and working. Therefore, there is no autonomous nature that stands apart from God, as a Deist world-machine or a purely isolated mechanical process. For the Spirit works in electrons and atoms as well as in mystical ecstasy. Hence there are no purely natural laws. This does not introduce a supernaturalism or magic into the cosmic process; rather, it means that what the scientist discovers as natural laws are manifestations of the energy of the cosmic Spirit. In this light, Darwin's principle of natural selection would be seen as a scientific way of charting the Spirit's selection of the species that will survive in the evolutionary process. Furthermore, the religious counselor cannot merely dismiss the findings of depth psychology as belonging to the "natural" realm; for even here in the depths of the unconscious, the Spirit works. In a theology of the cosmic Spirit, the theologian can see that at bottom there is no radical split between the sacred and the secular; for the Spirit works in the economic and political structures of society and in the ongoing scientific enterprise.

A theology of the cosmic Spirit leads to a problem. Its inherent optimism might distract us from the problem of evil in the world. We must be open to the Spirit and confident in the Spirit's ultimate victory. But this does not free us from the struggle with evil or the need for discernment of spirits. We must cooperate with the Spirit in the midst of a universe that is emerging from imperfection and that is shot through with the force of evil. Teilhard was acutely aware of the destructive power of evil, in turning love into hate, destroying unity, and leading to fragmentation, thus holding back the evolutionary process. In our times, there is great need for the gift of wisdom and discernment of spirits. Teilhard was sensitive to this problem and tried to determine some norms for judgment and decision making that would take into account the direction of evolution.[22]

I might illustrate the focus of our study by recasting the traditional hymn to the Holy Spirit *Veni, Creator Spiritus* ("Come, Creator Spirit") in the context of Teilhard's cosmic evolution. Written by Rabanus Maurus in the ninth century, the hymn begins:

> Come, Creator Spirit,
> Visit the minds of your own;
> Fill with divine grace
> The hearts you have created.[23]

We can recast the hymn to reflect both the traditional theology of the cosmic Spirit and Teilhard's own articulation of the emerging modern experience:

> Creative energy of the cosmos,
> Love that unites atoms and humans,
> That through convergence
> Creates new possibilities,
> Fill human consciousness
> With divine grace.
> Creative love energy,
> Infuse the divine milieu
> With energizing love
> And bring all creation
> To the completion of Omega.

CHAPTER FIVE

Teilhard de Chardin's Multicentric Model in Science and Theology: A Proposal for the Third Millennium

Ludovico Galleni

Introduction

In 1981, a delegation from Italy was invited to UNESCO head-quarters in Paris to celebrate the first centennial of the birth of Pierre Teilhard de Chardin. Discussions at that meeting stimulated our careful review and evaluation of his scientific papers. Since that time several conclusions have been reached.

Because of Teilhard's contributions to theories of evolution, a new model of interaction between science and theology is possible. His models compare to proposals by Averroes (Ibn Rush) in the Islamic world and by Galileo in the Western world (Galleni, 2002); moreover, one conclusion of our research led us to propose an environmental ethics that is based on Teilhard's vision of building the earth *in Christo Jesu* (Galleni and Scalfari, 2005; Ristori and Galleni, 2005).

Teilhard's scientific contribution to evolutionary theory clarified his redefinition of the term *orthogenesis* and its relationship to Darwinism and the so-called modern synthesis (Galleni, 1992). A further study included his definition of biology as the science of complexity with the proposal that a complete understanding of evolution is found in the study of the biosphere as a complex object (Galleni, 1995). A consequence of Teilhard's scientific understanding of the biosphere can be related to theology through his definitions of noosphere and biosphere (Galleni, 2001).

Nine letters written by Teilhard to his scientific mentor, Marcelin Boule, offered an interpretation of his broad research program (Galleni and Groessens Van Dyck, 2001). His proposal of the *moving toward* of matter in the direction of complexity, and of life toward consciousness, was investigated. His research program includes as main characteristics parallelisms and canalizations. He applied these characteristics of evolution to complexity processes in order to introduce a new science: geobiology. His study of long periods of time and large continental spaces interpreted convergence, not dispersion, to be the main characteristic of evolution. Fossil records supported his research program, which described the emergence of complexity and consciousness.

As with every scientific research program, Teilhard's vision encompasses a metaphysical component that is based on the literary meaning of *ta meta ta physika*, that is, the component of the program that is not based on the results of experiments or observations, but on the philosophical and religious sentiments of the scientists involved. Theology has a special role for humans in this vision of the universe. Humans are not just one species among others. Humans are essential to the arrow and task of evolution. Thus theology is essential for his new model of interaction between science and religion. It involves a human future on this planet that includes the final task of *moving toward*—convergence toward an Omega point, which is the moment of the second coming of Christ.

In view of a science of the biosphere that includes the *moving toward* of matter to complexity and an Omega point, there are ethical reasons to save the environment. A new environmental ethics is required in view of the scientific perspective developed by James Lovelock for planetary stability through symbiotic relationships between biosphere and noosphere. Teilhard's vision for building the earth *in Christo Jesu* can be discussed on the basis of the political proposal for fair trade (Ristori and Galleni, 2005) and in the thought of African statesman and poet, Leopold Sedar Senghor (Senghor, 1962).

The purpose of this essay is to present both a synthesis of the conclusions cited above, and avenues for future research.

A New Model of Interaction in Science-and-Theology

Based on the epistemological works of Imre Lakatos (Lakatos, 1978), we have proposed a new model of interaction between science and theology for the third millennium. The model is comparable to the Galilean model because theology is recovered in the process, and applied to construct a scientific theory. Lakatos had developed the falsification theory of Karl Popper and proposed that a scientific theory is something complex and cannot be falsified by a single crucial experiment. In order to underline his approach Lakatos does not speak of theories, but of scientific research programs. Scientific research programs are composed of two parts: a central core and a protective belt. The central core of a research program cannot be abandoned if the program is to survive. On the other hand, the protective belt offers indications about paths to be followed in order to further develop a theory. According to Lakatos, the central core of a scientific research program is formed not only by the results of observations and experiments, but also by a metaphysical component in the sense of the literal meaning of *ta meta ta physika*, as noted above. Discussion of the organization of the central core in our model here is of capital importance.

Our problem was to find Teilhard's scientific research program, and the composition of its central core. We know he considered himself primarily a scientist who was involved in the fields of geology, paleontology, and paleoanthropology. He is now considered the founder of modern paleontology of the Chinese subcontinent, and a member of the team that described the so-called Peking man. He was also a man of faith, who lived out his vocation in the Society of Jesus, known as the Jesuit order. In a page of his diary he compared his own vocation to that of Cardinal Newman, by assuming for himself the task of reconciling the church's doctrines with positive proposals from the modern world, primarily evolution. For example, he proposed paths of integration between evolutionary theory and Christian theology.

Side by side with the acceptance of evolution within Christian theology, he also attempted to recover for science some premises derived from theology. As a scientist, he was well aware of Darwinian mechanisms and of the casual interpretation of evolution. On the side of theology there was the suggestion to investigate the place of humans in nature, not as the result of a lucky event, but as necessary or a highly probable result of mechanisms that can be described by scientific laws.

The Making of the Program

In Teilhard's perspective of an evolutionary universe, time is irreversible, not cyclic. The duration of time includes the emergence of matter, of life, of animals, and finally of humans. Within the philosophical interpretation of so-called radical Darwinists, evolution cannot be just randomness and arbitrariness without any direction. Theology requires some necessity for the emergence of humans. As we have recently written, evolution must not simply be based alone on the law of change without any specific direction (see for this and the following topics: Gallen and Van Dyck, in press). Rather, evolution is a process of *moving toward* complexity and life, of life toward cerebralization, and of cerebralization toward a noosphere. Thus the biblical value of *moving toward* in the direction of humanity and further toward community, redemption, and salvation is placed inside the general movement of evolution.[1]

Experimental data in paleontology reveals canalization and parallelisms to be characteristic of the evolutionary mechanisms within Teilhard's research program. The research program proposed that geologists and paleontologists adopt new approaches and attitudes toward evolution. During the First World War his correspondence with Jean Boussac, professor of geology at the Institut catholique de Paris, reveals among other issues the necessity of taking a new approach to geology—a global approach. It is remarkable that a professor of geology suggested to the priest that he read the pages of a mystic, Angela da Foligno, that included her vision of God embedding the whole universe.[2] Teilhard adopted theology as an essential part of his scientific research program in which the central core was to find the hints of a *moving toward* complexity of matter, and of life toward cerebralization and the thinking creature. The hints were demonstrated by the presence of canalization and parallelisms that brought animal life toward cerebralization.

Thus the central core of the program was to look in fossil records for the presence of parallelisms and canalization as experimental evidence of the *moving toward* of evolution. The heuristic part of his program is found in his scientific papers. For example, after finishing his doctoral thesis he described the evolution of Tarsiers in a paper on the primates of the Quercy phosporites in southwest France. He wrote:

> So many harmonies in the similarities and differences lead us to think that Pseudoloris (its name should be Protarsius or Tarsiculus) belongs to the group that gives rise to the Tarsiers. Behind the Pseudolorises and the giant Pseudolorises, Tarsius, because of the development of its brain, occupies in a certain fashion among the Anaptomorphides a place that is symmetri-

cal with that held by man among the Anthropopoides.
(Teilhard de Chardin, 1971, 232)

and finally,

> Either because of some natural superiority or simply by
> chance, the simplification of the group of Tarsides,
> which was at first very dense, came about—and the
> greatest persistence was acquired—through a line that
> led to a larger brain.

A progressive expansion of the skull occurred. This is the
factor that dominates the history of the Tarsides (Teilhard de
Chardin, 1971, 239–40).

It is clear from these quotations that, even in his first scientific papers as a trained paleontologist, he looked for hints of a
general movement of animal evolution toward cerebralization. In
a paper presented at a meeting of the Institut français d'anthro-
pologie he noted:

> Considered in its entirety…the branch of the Anapto-
> morphides (or Tarsides) offers the case of an animal
> series that throughout the length of its history, through-
> out the development of varied and often divergent forms,
> is characterized by the ever increasing growth of its over-
> all size and diminution of its face to the profit of its brain.
> This evolutionary curve is worthy of attention: in effect it
> is following a process similar to, and as long and as com-
> plicated as, that which almost certainly produced the
> type Homo sapiens.
>
> The Hominiens are today considered by natural-
> ists either as a branch that was detached rather late
> from the group of anthropomorphic monkeys…or as a
> much earlier development born in the environs of that
> which produced the Tarsides….The very old individu-
> alization of the Tarsides and the parallelism that seems

to exist between their evolution and those of superior primates tends to support a third hypothesis, which could be expressed as follows: the three branches that respectively lead to man, to the Anthropomorphes and to Tarsier do not meet together at the interior of the Primates group as it is currently defined; rather, independently of each other, they grew out of a group still unknown of very small animals with a large brain that must have lived during the Paleocenic Age or even during an older period. (Teilhard de Chardin, 1971, 330)

This report is an example of the descriptive part of Teilhard's scientific research program, but for a great scientist, it was not enough. His research program required not only descriptions, but also mechanisms to explain observations. And here is the most fascinating part of Teilhard's scientific program. Although the description of parallelism and canalizations began with his first scientific papers, he found the best examples during his time in China. There he confirmed his difficulties with the reductionism approach of a neo-Darwinian interpretation and proposed the necessity of a different approach to study evolution, a global approach.

China was the best place to abandon a reductionism approach, and to look at evolution for broader mechanisms by taking a continental approach. The China experience was the great occasion in the scientific life of Teilhard, not only because of his papers on geology, paleontology, and paleoanthropology of the Chinese subcontinent, but also his contribution to the team that worked on the so-called Peking man. Moreover, his studies of continental evolution required a new scientific approach. As far as we know, he was the first scientist to propose continental evolution as the best way to develop a theory of complexity in biology. In one of his scientific papers Teilhard explained the opportunity for science, thanks to this "continental" approach:

It is always dangerous to generalize from particular observations. However, if we have not been misled by an arbitrary arrangement of facial features and fauna (an arbitrary and easy arrangement, because the facts available to us are too small in number), the considerations that proceed from them tend to establish that a careful study of animal transformations can only be pursued through the levels of a continent vast enough and old enough to have permitted the formation and the conservation of a "specifically continental" fauna.

If we don't take the precaution to make a selection of such a zoological group, the phenomena of evolution will infallibly mask the internal variations of Life under external appearances. On the contrary, if we study a continental stock, such as we have defined it, the perplexities of a "cryptogenic" origin are nearly eliminated; in this case, the organic rhythm of evolution—its true rhythm—is discovered in its pure state. (Reprinted in: P. Teilhard de Chardin, 1971, 866–67)

Writing from China to a scientist-friend, he proposed one of the first definitions of complexity (Teilhard de Chardin, 1967, 251):

I could be very tempted to bring in at the origin of the branches, at the forks, biological causes of a special kind, the subject of which would not be individuals but more or less important parts of the biosphere. In all sciences it seems to me that we give-in far too much to the illusion that all phenomena can be represented on a small scale or can be explained only by the elements. But only in geometry do figures keep the properties while decreasing. Natural groups of living beings must have properties which living beings taken separately are missing. —I hope to see a biology of the biosphere such as we are starting to have a chemistry of the lithosphere.

It is clear that the whole is incomprehensible if one looks only at its parts, by following methods of reductionism. Moreover, reductionism is unable to describe all the mechanisms of evolution.

The necessity of a new approach to biology that is related to a global vision of geology and evolution began early in the development of Teilhard's thought. The approach is documented in the exchange of letters during the First World War with Jean Boussac, referred to above. Both of these scientists discussed the limitation of a reductionism, and agreed on a global approach to geological and biological events in evolution. Canalization and parallelisms, examples of the *moving toward* of evolution, would become more evident in a large-scale investigation. Thus the necessity to describe laws to explain the emergence of humans, suggested to Teilhard by theology, required that he develop a method to study increasing biological complexity.

Biology as the Science of Complexity

Teilhard studied the biosphere through the evolution of complexity. The metaphysical component of his scientific research program, that is the *moving toward* of evolution, was shown by experimental and theoretical data. His global approach came about by investigation of the whole biosphere as a complex object. He found canalization and parallelisms to be the result of evolution of the biosphere. They were the protective belt of his research program. His interest was not limited to increases in cerebral size, but in every kind of parallelism. After the organization of his research program by the end of the 1930s, he found the best examples of parallelisms in the evolution of mole rats during the Chinese Pleistocene (Galleni and Groessens Van Dyck, in press).

Teilhard's definition of contemporary biology as the science of complexity was suggested by the necessity of theology. This vision led to his study of mechanisms of evolution at the level of the whole biosphere, and the foundation of the new science of geobiology.

The Science of the Biosphere

The two starting points for geobiology were: (1) all living beings belong to a single system in which the elements are organically interdependent, and taken as a whole are bound to the surface of the earth; (2) these organic sheets were not physically separable from the general mass of the earth that they cover.

Thus geobiology investigates the internal functioning of the biosphere, and at the same time determines the functional and structural place that the biosphere occupies within the system of the other envelopes of the earth. Geobiology's final task is to find laws that permit the general process of *moving toward* complexity and the emergence of life and consciousness. The result of the methodology of geobiology is descriptions of fossil records from the perspective of long periods of time and on a large scale (the continental one) of parallelisms and canalization. Here are the proofs that evolution was mainly a *moving toward* complexity and consciousness. The model verifies the role of theology that suggested to science new methods and discoveries.

At this point we can summarize the scientific research program of Teilhard de Chardin: The central core of evolution is not a casual dispersion of evolutionary branches, but a convergence toward cerebralization. This summary is brought out in a comment by Teilhard regarding a book by George Gaylord Simpson, the American scientist who brought paleontology inside the perspective of the modern synthesis (reprinted in P. Teilhard de Chardin, 1971, 4287):

> In the course of these developments, Dr. Simpson maintained right to the end the intransigent attitude of the neo-Darwinists, which his friends knew he held.
>
> This view believed that everything in zoological evolution could be explained by the play of selective chance

68

alone. Despite incontestable advantages to this attitude (such as the biologist's obligation to analyze and demonstrate thoroughly the mechanisms of morphogenesis), we repeat once again that there is an obvious weakness. In its determination to close its eyes to the indisputable psychic development ("invention") that universally accompanies the expansion and arrangement of the biosphere, it removes all direction and global significance from the process of evolution, with the particularly disturbing result of leaving unexplained and scientifically incomprehensible the human phenomenon.

We have often quoted this paragraph because it relates clearly to our thesis. In every scientific research program there is a central core that contains a metaphysical component. Whereas Simpson proposes neo-Darwinism and modern synthesis based on the metaphysics of chance, he denies any peculiar direction in evolution. On the other hand, Teilhard's notion of evolution is *moving toward* complexity and consciousness. Today, this *moving toward* notion is generally accepted. For example, canalization and parallelisms are considered main aspects of evolution in recent books written by eminent paleontologists, Mark McMenamin (McMenamin, 1998) and Simon Conway Morris (Conway Morris, 2003).

The necessity of theology is at the center of Teilhard's model for the science-religion relationship. It suggested the construction of a new scientific research program in which biology is the science of complexity of the biosphere and of life. Following general systems theory, the biosphere is considered to be a complex system whose parts are connected in order to maintain stability of the system. Stability is a relatively new concept developed in Lovelock's papers following Vernadsky's and Teilhard's concept of a biosphere. In Teilhard's scientific writings we find the description of canalization and parallelisms as a result of the mechanisms of evolution of the biosphere. In Lovelock's writings we find the description of stability of the major variables that allow the biosphere to survive and life to evolve.

A primary consequence of Teilhard's scientific perspective is that the biosphere acts as a gigantic thermodynamic machine. As first suggested by Vernadsky, solar energy continually makes possible the process of evolution, which is in Teilhard's a *moving toward* complexity and consciousness (Teilhard's contribution). This astonishing aspect of the movement of life inside the biosphere maintains the stability of the variables that allow it to survive. However, the *moving toward* of human activity is acting against stability and this is the main difference between nature's activity and the human activity that is now putting at risk the capacity of life to survive on planet Earth.

Symbiosis

Symbiosis is a concept to consider when evaluating the stability of the biosphere and instability of the noosphere. In the early twentieth century the Lotka-Volterra equation for predator-prey relationships described for the first time a mathematical model of survival among animal species.

Umberto D'Ancona, a zoologist and son-in-law of Volterra, continued the development in a book that explained relationships inside the ecosystem. D'Ancona described the biosphere as a gigantic biological association, just as Vernardsky spoke of the biosphere as a gigantic thermodynamic machine (D'Ancona, 1942). It is interesting that D'Ancona's book was first published in a series of volumes dedicated to "*exacten Biologie*," and edited by Ludwig von Bertalanffy, who after the Second World War founded general systems theory in the United States.[3]

Piero Leonardi, a zoologist who received his degree at Padua with D'Ancona, was the first Italian scientist to promulgate the ideas of Teilhard de Chardin. In a book on biological evolution he presented a general theory that suggested the presence of symbiotic relationships among organisms side by side in the biosphere, which compose the ecosystem (Leonardi, 1950). We propose therefore that it is possible to trace back to Teilhard, thanks to an Italian scientist (Leonardi), the topic of symbiosis. This symbiotic perspective, which was taken up by Lynn Margulis, inside the scientific research program of Lovelock's Gaia hypothesis, is rich in its developments (Margulis, 1998).

Perspectives and Suggestions for Future Research: Building the Earth *in Christo Jesu*

In Teilhard's papers there is another development that can be considered a center of intersection between science and theology: the investigation about a final task of evolution and of its *moving toward*. Science has suggested that human evolution in the future will be different than that of other species: no longer divergence, but convergence. A consequence of the evolution of the brain has been the emergence of the thinking creature and the presence of a new entity in the universal economy, the noosphere. The argument is well developed elsewhere (Galleni and Scalfari, 2005) and it is not necessary to go again into its birth and the significance Teilhard gave to it.

Thinking creatures have developed cultures, new aspects of evolution, that allow for rapid transmission of acquired characteristics. These cultures permit a strong element of linkage among individuals, groups, and societies. According to Teilhard, evolutionary mechanisms of divergence and speciation, typical of other animal species, stopped at the human level. On the contrary, human populations in evolution have moved toward convergence. Teilhard developed this important point for theology in the book that he called his "pious book," *Le milieu divin*.

In Teilhard's theological perspective, convergence had a final task: *moving toward* the Omega point, the moment for the second coming of Christ. This purely theological concept cannot be investigated by evolutionary biologists, such as myself.[4] But it is of general interest that this perspective of Teilhard's again gave to Christianity a task in this world. Terrestrial realities are not only places to exert virtues in order to find salvation in paradise. In Teilhard's theology, they become instruments for the eschatological movement of humanity in this world toward the Omega point. This is a path of communion on the earth that brings forth a reevaluation of terrestrial realities. This path, clearly a revolution in Christian understanding of reality, was recovered in the document of the Second Vatican Council, *Gaudium et Spes* (The Church in the Modern World).

In Teilhard's perspective it is incumbent on a human being to preserve the natural background that allows his/her *moving toward*. The task can be performed only if the biosphere is preserved. After Teilhard de Chardin, environmental ethics will be a fundamental chapter in moral theology. But how can the theological value of the biosphere be preserved? This is a matter for science.

The development of our understanding of the biosphere gave rise to a theory of its stability that was proposed by James Lovelock. As a system, the biosphere presents mechanisms of control that can maintain stability of those variables that permit survival of life on earth. Maintenance of stability of the biosphere is the tool that permits human survival for the performance of its theological task. Thus stability of the biosphere acquires theological value, thanks to the vision acquired by environmental ethics.

The Noosphere

We have introduced the concept of the biosphere as the global concept that represents living beings at the planetary level. But how can we manage the global activity of humans? Again, we go to Teilhard and the introduction of his concept of the noosphere. The definition of the noosphere has been taken from one of his last scientific papers, published posthumously in 1955

(Teilhard de Chardin, 1971, 4580–89). There he provides a definition, "...the psychically reflexive human surface, for which, together with Professor Edouard LeRoy and Professor Vernadsky, we suggested in the 1920s the name 'noosphere'" (Teilhard de Chardin, 1971, 4581). The concept refers to all humans and their peculiar talents of reflection and self-consciousness.

At the birth of the noosphere, the rising and diffusion of the thinking creature brought about a new kind of evolution in which cultural characteristics were transmitted more quickly than genetic inheritance. After the early period when humans evolved primarily in Africa, there was a rapid spreading over the surface of the earth during the Upper Paleolithic period. These migrations were not for ecological or adaptive reasons; rather, quite probably, they were related to the need for knowledge or, at least, to the curiosity of thinking creatures. The result of this human movement was a new and peculiar form of evolution that was characterized not by acquiring different genes, but by the establishment of distinct cultures, and the interaction of those cultures.

> For the many fragments of mankind that have become isolated or have gained their independence in the course of time, just so many tentative technomental systems of the world as a whole—that is, just so many—have gradually come into existence. This is one of the major lessons taught by universal human history, from the earliest known stages until the present time. (Teilhard de Chardin, 1971, 4584)

Global instruments like the noosphere are needed in a global situation. Moreover, an ethical perspective is required to manage the activities of the noosphere toward the biosphere. Therefore we look again at the Gaia hypothesis, and to a second concept that is at the basis of the Gaia hypothesis, namely symbiosis.

We have discussed symbiosis after the proposal of Lynn Margulis, which is considered now to be one of the most important and extensive mechanisms of evolution (Gallen, 2003). We concluded that symbiosis is the key mechanism that allows life to survive in extreme environments. Symbiosis is also the mechanism that allows life to pass the threshold between prokaryotic and eukaryotic beings. According to Margulis, symbiosis is a set of ecological interactions between organisms, thanks to protracted physical associations of one or more members of different species (Margulis, 1991). Associations between partners would be significant to the well-being or the "unwell-being" of one or both of the participants.

Symbiosis has been used with a wider meaning by Leonardi (Leonardi, 1950) to describe connections inside the biosphere. Taking into consideration these approaches to symbiosis we may ask the question: Is it correct to use the term *symbiosis* to describe relationships between noosphere and biosphere? The term is used here to relate a physical association among spheres in which the partnerships at present are tightly integrated. Moreover, associations are significant for the well-being or "unwell-being" of one or both participants. Symbiosis exists when two living entities are sharing the same task. Stability of the variables that allows for survival may be the common task shared by both of the participants, biosphere and noosphere.

We now have a framework to manage ethical activities of the noosphere with regard to the biosphere. The activities must be symbiotic because both spheres are necessary to maintain stability in the biosphere, and therefore to protect the environment that the noosphere shares. Every aspect of moral activity by humans can be evaluated within the context of stability of the biosphere. Any inquiry of environmental ethics that does not include biosphere stability is meaningless. Therefore the relationships between noosphere and biosphere require a final consideration: How should the noosphere develop in order to realize *moving toward*?

Investigations of the biosphere itself have suggested that stability of its main variables, which permit evolution and the survival of life, occur through the progressive diffusion of diversity. Diversity and stability are strictly connected, and both are mechanisms for survival of the biosphere. Stability is also maintained, thanks to diversity. We know that general variables like temperature, seawater salinity, carbon dioxide, and oxygen levels in the biosphere have remained stable, at least in the last hundreds of million years. The question is asked, what are the general variables to be maintained in the noosphere? Is it possible to develop a parallelism between the general variables of the biosphere and the noosphere?

Obviously, significant general variables for the noosphere are not physical. They are social and political, and have been published in the United Nations Declaration of Human Rights. Today there is wide discussion about diversity, and how the Western concept of democracy could be expanded. Following some papers of Teilhard concerned with the creation and development of the United Nations, it is our opinion that human populations that are rich in cultural diversity must be maintained. Human cultures are complementary, and can represent richness in the noosphere that will support its stability. There is need for general agreement about values that must be preserved everywhere and by every culture. These values can be found in the United Nations Declaration of Human Rights.

In these tragic years we need wide discussion about diversity in the noosphere. The concept of diversity includes the richness of cultural diversity. Some general values must be respected everywhere in order to build an earth that includes biosphere and noosphere. A political proposal by the former president of Senegal, Leopold Sedar Senghor, expressly referred to the political vision of Teilhard de Chardin.[5] Senghor followed Teilhard when he wrote that the best mechanisms to preserve a noosphere with its richness and diversity will be based on a polycentric organization. Cultural life will pass from individuals to communities, and then to villages, cities, and nations.

Today we have a unique model that continues to progressively extend its influence and culture on the earth. A different model is needed and Teilhard's vision could be useful. New perspectives for humans within the vision of Senghor include economic relationships, such as fair trade agreements.

Conclusion

We have found in the model of interactions suggested by Teilhard de Chardin a multifocus model. The model has many points of contact and includes reciprocal relationships and mutual influences between science and theology. The model represents a perspective and possibilities for the third millennium.

References

Conway Morris, Simon, 2003. *Life's Solution*, Cambridge, Cambridge University Press.

D'Ancona, Umberto, 1942. *La lottaper L'esistenza*, Einaudi Torino, 1942.

Galleni, Ludovico, 1992. "Relationships between scientific analysis and the world view of Pierre Teilhard de Chardin." *Zygon*, 27, 153–66.

Galleni, Ludovico, 1995. "How does the teilhardian vision of evolution compare with contemporary theories." *Zygon*, 30, 25–45.

Galleni, Ludovico, 1998. *Aspetti teorici della biologia evoluzionistica*, in: P. Freguglia ed., *Modelli matematici nelle Scienze Biologiche*, Quattro Venti, Urbino, 11–66.

Galleni, Ludovico, 2001. "Is Biosphere doing Theology?" *Zygon*, 36, 33–48.

Galleni, Ludovico, 2002. *"Scienza-e-teologia, it progetto del terzo millennia."* Postfazione a: V. Maraldi, Lo Spirito Creatore e la novita del cosmo, ed. Paoline, Milano, 2002, 251–79.

Galleni, Ludovico, 2003. *The Challenge of Biotechnology to Christian Anthropology: A Western (Mediterranean) Perspective*, in: (V. Gekas ed.) *Christian Anthropology and Biotechnological Progress*, Technical University of Crete, Chania, 61–74.

Galleni, Ludovico, et Marie Claire Groessens-Van Dyck, 2001. "Lettres d' un paleontologue. Neuf lettres inedites de Pierre Teilhard de Chardin a Marcellin Boule," *Revue des questions scientifiques* 172, 5–104.

Galleni, Ludovico, et Marie Claire Groessens-Van Dyck (in press). *A Model of Interaction Between Science and Theology Based on the Scientific Papers of Pierre Teilhard de Chardin*, In: *Knowledge, Science, and Religion: Philosophical Investigations*, edited by William Sweet and Richard Feist.

Galleni, Ludovico, and Scalfari Francesco, 2005. "Teilhard de Chardin's engagement with the Relationship between Science and Theology in Light of Discussions about Environmental Ethics." *Ecotheology*, 10.2, 196–214.

Lakatos, Imre, 1978. *The Methodology of Scientific Research Programs*, in *Philosophical Papers*, vol. 1, J. Worral and G. Currie ed. Cambridge, Cambridge University Press.

Leonardi, Piero, 1950. *L'evoluzione dei viventi*, Morcelliana, Brescia.

McMenamin, Marc, 1998. *The Garden of Ediacara*. Columbia University Press, New York.

Margulis, Lynn, 1991. *Symbiogenesis and Symbionticism*, in: *Symbiosis as a Source of Evolutionary Innovation*, L. Margulis and R. Fetser, eds., 1–14.

Margulis, Lynn, 1998. *Symbiotic Planet*, Basic Books, New York.

Martelet, Gustav, 2005. *Teilhard de Chardin, prophéte d'un Christ toujours plus grand*. Lessius, Bruxelles.

Ruse, Michael, 1996. *From Monad to Man*, Cambridge University Press.

Ristori, Stefano, and Ludovico Galleni, 2005. "Models of ethical acting. The air trade agriculture as an example of sustainable development and respect of Cultures, Nature and Human Rights." *European Journal of Science and Theology*, 1(3)11–25 (2005).

Senghor, Leopold Sedar. 1962. "Pierre Teilhard de Chardin et la politique africaine," *Cahiers Pierre Teilhard de Chardin*, 13–65.

Senghor, Leopold Sedar, 1968. "Hommage a Pierre Teilhard de Chardin pour le 10e anniversaire de sa mort," *Cahiers Pierre Teilhard de Chardin*, 6, 29–35.

Teilhard de Chardin, Pierre, 1967. "Lettres inédites à un savant de ses amis," *Christus*, 14, 251.

Teilhard de Chardin, Pierre, 1971. *L'oeuvre scientifique*, K. and N. Schmitz Moormann ed. Walter-Verlag, Freiburg in Breisgrau.

Teilhard de Chardin, Pierre, 1975. *Journal, 26 aout 1915, 4 janvier 1919*. Fayard, Paris.

Teilhard de Chardin, Pierre, et Jean Boussac, 1986. *Lettres de guerre inédites*, O.E.I.L., Paris.

CHAPTER SIX

Teilhard's Spiritual Vision of the Mystical Milieu

Philip Hefner

"The bread of the Eucharist is stronger than our flesh."
Gregory of Nyssa

Writing in Tientsin, China, on March 25, 1924, Teilhard produced his second essay to bear the title "My Universe." This piece has long held a special meaning for me. Its ideas are magnetic; they draw us into a breathtaking view of God and the world. What first attracted me to this essay and what has remained with me, finding expression in my preaching and teaching, is the eucharistic image that carries Teilhard's vision. Citing Gregory of Nyssa, he writes, "The bread of the Eucharist is stronger than our flesh; that is why it is the bread that assimilates us, and not we the bread, when we receive it." The bread, which is the body of Christ, consumes us. We know that Teilhard understood the entire created world to be the eucharistic host. It is this host that is elevated in Teilhard's striking version of the Eucharist—*The Mass on the World*. The body of Christ is situated by the host that we receive in the sacramental ritual, but it is not confined there. The Eucharist has "real and physical extensions":

> Since Christ is above all omega, that is, the universal "form" of the world, he can attain his organic balance and plenitude only by mystically assimilating all that sur-

rounds him. The Host is like a blazing hearth from which flames spread their radiance. Just as the spark that falls into the heather is soon surrounded by a wide circle of fire, so the sacramental Host of bread is continually being encircled more closely by another, infinitely larger, Host, which is nothing less than the universe itself....The world is the final, and the real, Host into which Christ gradually descends until his time is fulfilled.[1]

With these words, Teilhard has given us a striking image of the Eucharist, one that impresses itself indelibly in our minds. The image embodies an entire worldview, a vision of the natural world in relation to Christ and, through Christ, to the purposes of God, since for Teilhard assimilation into the eucharistic host is incorporation, not into a static state of blessedness, but rather into a process—the world's transformation and movement toward the fulfillment that God purposes for the creation. In this essay, I intend to probe this eucharistic imagery and the vision that comes to expression in the image. The focus of my probing is the texts of "My Universe" and *The Divine Milieu*,[2] and I will try wherever possible to let those texts speak for themselves in the words of their author. We must keep in mind that in elaborating this theme, Teilhard was at his most intimate and personal; the vision of the mystical milieu represents his own way of dealing with the issues of his own professional and personal life; it is his own construction—the synthesis which he forged for his own life.

Alerting Us to the Future

It scarcely needs saying that Teilhard was an extraordinary person. One facet of his remarkable character is the extent to which he was in touch with the fundamental currents of his time, early and mid-twentieth century. He was so deeply in touch that he was ahead of most of his contemporaries. We might apply the term *seer* to Teilhard, and what he saw was rooted in his own personal experience. When we look back, fifty years after his death, we are led to the judgment that in his sensibilities he was in effect an early distant alerting system, describing the emerging intellectual and spiritual landscape that he discerned from his own life and work and alerting us to its significance. It is a landscape that even now, although it is familiar to the leading edge of society, escapes the notice of far too many of us. Teilhard not only perceived the flow of life and history in his time, he knew that that flow defined who he was. He spoke for the sake of his fellow humans, to be sure, but he also expressed what he knew he himself needed for his life. He speaks of the one "fact that will remain permanently unchallenged: that an ordinary man of the twentieth century, because he shared as any one else would in the ideas and cares of his own time, has been unable to find the proper balance for his interior life except in a unitary concept, based upon physics, of the world and Christ."[3] He identified himself with this "ordinary man," and in the essay "My Universe" he aims to present such a unitary concept. He sets forth his own personal confession:

A spiritual urge has been trying to express itself in me, which others, later, will pin down more felicitously. I feel, indeed, that it is not that I conceived this essay: it is a man within me who is greater than I....For all its limitations, my experience in these last ten years has convinced me that both within and outside Christianity many more minds than we suspect are drawing nourishment from the same intuitions and the same ill-defined feelings as those that have filled my life. It has been my destiny to stand at a privileged cross-roads in the world; there, in my twofold character of priest and scientist, I have felt passing through me, in particularly exhilarating and varied conditions, the double stream of human and divine forces....I feel that I would be disloyal to Life, disloyal,

too, to those who need my help, if I did not try to
describe to them the features of the resplendent image
that has been disclosed to me in the universe in the
course of twenty-five years of reflexions and experiences
of all sorts.[4]

Teilhard knew that a growing number of people are conscious of themselves as "being an atom or a citizen of the universe."[5] He knew himself to be such a citizen. In *The Divine
Milieu*, he describes these citizens more simply as "those whose
education or instinct leads them to listen primarily to the voices
of the earth."[6] For such people, talk of life's meaning, of basic values, and of transcendence or God had to engage their identity as
citizen-atoms of the universe. Let us remind ourselves once more
of what he considers to be essential for maintaining such citizenship: *finding the proper balance for one's interior life in a unitary
concept, based upon physics, of the world and Christ.*

We might put Teilhard's insight into different—today widely
accepted—usage, by saying that ordinary people increasingly
understand themselves in naturalistic terms; some form of that
perspective that we often call *naturalism* is indigenous to contemporary worldviews. The engine that drives the new worldview is
scientific discovery.

While for some, this new knowledge is cause to rejoice, for
others it raises deep anxieties. For some the vastness of the universe
that is now revealed makes humans seem so insignificant that they
"no longer count"; for others the world as we now understand it is
so beautiful that "it, and it alone, must be adored." These people
who have newly recognized themselves as atoms and citizens of the
universe often "have a certain fear that they may be false to themselves or diminish themselves if they simply follow the Gospel
path."[7] Teilhard gives eloquent voice to this anxiety:

Is the Christ of the Gospels, imagined and loved within
the dimensions of a Mediterranean world, capable of

still embracing and still forming the centre of our prodigiously expanded universe? Is the world not in the process of becoming more vast, more close, more dazzling than Jehovah? Will it not burst our religion asunder? Eclipse our God?[8]

Today the situation that Teilhard pointed to is even clearer, both in its breadth and in its urgency. Countless writers, some of them distinguished scientists, embody the effort to forge worldviews that exclude any reality apart from the natural order. Distinctions between the natural and the supernatural are rendered impossible and unnecessary within the framework of such thinking.[9] Christian writers recognize the point of this critique and attempt to meet it in their own ways.[10]

Teilhard felt the urgency, both in his own life and in that of others ("as I know from having come across them all over the world," he writes[11]), and he met it head-on. As we have already noted, he sought to shape a *unitary* concept that rests on the description of the world that we gain from the physical sciences, and that includes the presence of God and Christ. He did not exempt his thinking from the bottom-line force of physics—we remember that by the time he had written "My Universe" in 1924, Max Planck, Albert Einstein, and Niels Bohr had already received the Nobel Prize, and the work of Louis de Broglie, Werner Heisenberg, Erwin Schrödinger, and Paul Dirac, all of whom would receive the prize in the next few years, was well known. He sought a description of God's presence in the world that was not only unitary, but that possessed as well "solid, natural, total coherence."[12]

The dualism between nature and supernature was rendered unnecessary. Invoking St. Paul's speech on the Areopagus (Acts 17:22–31), he writes that "God is as pervasive and perceptible as the atmosphere in which we are bathed. He encompasses us on all sides, like the world itself."[13] Skepticism, fears, and anxiety are due to our "inability *to see him*." Teilhard constructs his coherent description as a way to overcome that inability.

In Eo Vivimus—The Mystical Milieu

Teilhard presents the conceptual formulation of this coherent description in his celebrated theory of complexity-consciousness. This theory describes the evolutionary movement of the natural world from the origins of matter toward ever greater complexity—which he defines as increasing unity that supports ever more intense individuation—that culminates in the Omega Point, which is God's fulfillment of the creation in Christ. However, in "My Universe" and *The Divine Milieu*, as Teilhard himself writes, he does not present a philosophical-theological conceptuality; rather, he is offering a description located psychologically—a *"psychological* evolution observed *over a specified interval*...inward perspectives gradually revealed to the mind in the course of a humble yet 'illuminative' spiritual ascent."[14] These texts present what a mystic feels with his entire being.

With this as his intention, Teilhard chooses the term *milieu* to articulate his unitary concept. As his translator reminds us, the French term implies "center and environment or setting." We should reflect for a moment on the choice of the term *milieu*. At the outset, Teilhard made it clear that the interior life is at the center of his concern. The ordinary man of the twentieth century who shares in the ideas and cares of the current times seeks "proper balance for his interior life." Teilhard speaks of his empathy with those who, having listened to the voices of earth, fear that they will be "false to themselves or diminish themselves." He emphasizes that he is focusing on the psychological dimension; we might add, in today's terminology, that *spirituality* is the realm of his concern in these writings.

We note also that even though Teilhard speaks of the interior life—his own and that of others—his unitary descriptive concept speaks first of all not of the contours of individual life, although he certainly does consider these contours, but rather of that of which the individual is a part, that to which the individual belongs that is greater than the individual—the *milieu*. He spoke movingly of his own intimate belonging to the milieu, and this belonging defined his own citizenship in the universe. He called this the *mystical milieu* and also the *divine milieu*.

Teilhard could have employed other images. He could have spoken of God as "other," as a personal reality that stands over against us and encounters us in our lives. Protestant theology is particularly accustomed to such imagery. Another image might have been God as creative ground of our being, from which we emerge, and the foundation of our lives. Teilhard includes God as both "other" and as creative ground in his purview, but the driving image is that to which we belong and in which we live our lives—the ambience that envelops us and permeates us.

Let us consider how he described his perception of the milieu and his belonging:

> All around us, to the right and left, in front and behind, above and below, we have only had to go a little beyond the frontier of sensible appearances in order to see the divine welling up and showing through. But it is not only close to us, in front of us, that the divine presence has revealed itself. It has sprung up so universally, and we find ourselves so surrounded and transfixed by it, that there is no room left to fall down and adore it, even within ourselves. By means of all created things, without exception, the divine assails us, penetrates us and moulds us. We imagined it as distant and inaccessible, whereas in fact we live steeped in its burning layers. *In eo vivimus.*[15]

In the foregoing, Teilhard speaks in terms of milieu as environment or ambience. We noted earlier the translator's reminder that milieu can also be translated as "center." Teilhard speaks in this vein when he writes, in words that are in effect extensions of his depiction of the eucharistic host:

God reveals himself everywhere, beneath our groping efforts, *as a universal milieu*, only because he is *the ultimate point* upon which all realities converge. Each element of the world, whatever it may be, only subsists, *hic et nunc*, in the manner of a cone whose generatrices meet in God who draws them together…all created things, every one of them, cannot be looked at, in their nature and action, without the same reality being found in their innermost being—like sunlight in the fragments of a broken mirror.[16]

Because God is center, he is infinitely near and yet also dispersed throughout the material world. As center, God "fills the whole sphere."

Teilhard set great store by his theory of creative union, which undergirds the idea of milieu as a center. Evolution proceeds by "union of elements into higher unities in which something new comes into existence."[17] Since he believed that God is the creator of the world that proceeds by means of evolution, he formulated his theory that to be created is to be united out of many: "*esse=plus plura unire* (to be=to unite more the many)."[18] This principle of creative union applies to the physical and biological realms, as well as to human society. The process of union is also redemption. This redemption includes both the whole of the universe and its individuals, because union is not the absorption or dissolution of the individuals, but rather their intensification. Two familiar aphorisms have been used to convey these Teilhardian ideas: "Everything that rises must converge" and "union differentiates."

"The Mystical Milieu Is a Flesh"

The milieu is fully material—it would have to be to serve as the unitary descriptive concept that Teilhard intends. "If we had to give a more exact name to the mystical Milieu we would say that it is a Flesh—for it has all the properties the flesh has of palpable domination and limitless embrace."[19] It is the world, and as a result "not one of the impressions I receive from it fails to inform me a little more about God. Like a powerful organism, the world transforms me into him who animates it."[20] With these words, Teilhard opens a window for us to see a powerful spiritual vision that has immense practical possibilities. Union with Christ and union with the world become one process of growth—physically, morally, and spiritually. Christ and the world are inseparable. We recognize this as the pervasive Teilhardian emphasis on "Christogenesis"—the full participation of Christ in the evolutionary dynamic of the world. This theme is, as we shall see, also the dominant motif of his eucharistic imagery as well as his spiritual classic, *The Divine Milieu*.

Three threads are particularly important for Teilhard as he elaborates the process of Christogenesis: the materiality of the process, its placement within the incarnation, and its dynamic of creative union. The materiality factor coalesces with the incarnation in that Christ, following St. Paul, holds all things together and brings them into a whole (Col 1:17). The "power of the Word Incarnate penetrates matter itself; it goes down into the deepest depths."[21] The incarnation, like creation and even the divine, is not a final, finished reality, but a continuing process leading to transformation. "We are constantly forgetting that the supernatural is a ferment, a soul, and not a complete and finished organism."[22] We are incorporated into this process, from our own very beginnings in this cosmic process that Christ permeates. We are not finished organisms, either. Our origins are in the cosmos. In order to possess our own humanity, we must recognize these roots of our being: They "plunge back and down into the unfathomable past."[23] Christ is incarnated in it all, and thus he and the material order he permeates can also be designated as the mystical milieu in which we have our being.

God Creates through Natural Physical Processes

This motif is, characteristically, expressed by Teilhard in terms of his personal mystical vision, embodied in primal Christian symbol and ritual, and clothed in the language of spirituality. I have noted that Teilhard's presentation of this vision grows out of his most intimate personal spiritual experience. He intentionally eschews philosophical conceptual language. Nevertheless, his articulation of the vision also speaks to the intellect; it contains a powerful conceptual interpretation of the world, including the natural world, our life in the world, and God's presence in the world. It is to this intellectual-conceptual dimension that I want to draw particular attention.

"My Universe" elaborates Teilhard's personal engagement with the natural world through the medium of his experience both as a Catholic Christian and Jesuit priest and as a scientist. His Christian faith told him that nature is God's creation, a gift from God, and a resource for enriching life. His scientific work told him that this gift from God is shaped in an evolutionary mold. His is clearly a post-Darwinian worldview, in that evolution is at the center of his understanding of nature. His coherent concept reconciles "scientific views on evolution (accepted as, in their essence, definitively established) with the innate urge that has impelled me to look for the Divine through matter, and, in some sort of way, in union with matter."[24] This view extends his awareness that, in addition to its character as gift and resource, nature shapes us; it makes us who we are. God's work of creation is exercised through the agencies of the evolutionary forces that he understood in his education and research as a geologist and paleontologist. We are embodied in the natural world. Its elements and processes, like the warp and woof of a tapestry on the loom, weave the fiber that constitutes our personhood and the lives that we lead. The flesh of the mystical milieu is nature's evolution, which "transforms me into" the God who "animates" that nature. It is central to Teilhard's vision that God's intention for the creation is expressed in a medium that is evolutionary in character. He concentrated his work on elaborating this expression. Karl Schmitz-Moormann has called attention to Teilhard's idea of "God's diaphany" in the evolutionarily configured creation.[25]

Christians are accustomed to speaking of the creation as gift and resource. Creation is God's gift to us, and as such it can be a realm of grace. It is also resource for our lives, providing us with the conditions of life, food, shelter, material for our technical achievements, and spiritual growth. We recognize that we have often in human history distorted creation as resource, exploiting it to support our desires, over and above our needs, as well as our greed. Teilhard recognized both the gift and resource character of nature, but he went beyond them to a third motif—the physical world as agency of God's creation, including the creation of our human selves and lives.

Rooting God's creating work in the creative processes of nature itself finds an echo in the first chapter of Genesis, where God commands the earth itself to create vegetation and animals. In verse 11, we read, "Then God said, let the earth put forth vegetation," and in verse 20, "Let the waters bring forth swarms of living creatures." As Wolfhart Pannenberg has interpreted this passage of scripture:

> God does not need to create all by himself and alone but recruits the assistance of his creatures. In affirming that the earth brought forth not only primitive forms of life but even higher animals, the Bible is more audacious than Darwin was....The use of the earth as agency in God's work of creation is significant...especially when connected with the idea of a continuing divine activity of creation, as suggested by other biblical passages.[26]

Teilhard himself provides both a commentary and an elaboration of this vision in his work, *The Divine Milieu*. This essay bears the motto taken, of course, from the Gospel of John (3:16):

Sic Deus Dilexit Mundum
For those who love the world

The Divine Milieu is structured in two major sections: "the divinization of our activities" and "the divinization of our passivities." In choosing this structure, Teilhard intended to cover the whole of the "interior life." His argument is that our immersion in the material world is at the same time an immersion in God. His thinking is, he says, an interpretation of St. Paul's words: "whether we live or whether we die, we are the Lord's" (Rom 14:8): "By means of all created things, without exception, the divine assails us, penetrates us and moulds us"—that is a central motif of the vision of "my universe" that Teilhard sets before us. This takes place in a double rhythm: On the one hand we are shaped by the material world and on the other we shape the world, and in both segments of this rhythm God is shaping us.

These energies mold the most intimate life of our being—body and soul, and the two are inseparable. The body does not develop independent of the soul, and the soul cannot grow apart from the body. The "human soul, however independently created our philosophy represents it as being, is inseparable, in its birth and in its growth, from the universe into which it is born."[27] This happens to us as passive recipient of energies we do not control, but we, too, play a role; "we must industriously assemble the widely scattered elements."[28] We are obedient and docile recipients and also faithful builders of both our bodies and our souls.

Both our activities and our passivities are instruments of God's molding through material, earthly means. Matter presents itself to us as both "burden" and "exuberance."[29] As burden, matter weighs us down; it is the source of pain, sin, and threat; it paralyzes us and renders us vulnerable. But it is also exuberance—ennobling, the "joy of growth," nourishment; it lifts us up; "to be deprived of it is intolerable." Teilhard likens our interactions with matter to a climber on a fog-bound mountainside, struggling upwards toward the summit. The climber is shrouded and unable to see the peak, which is bathed in bright sunlight. The matter that constitutes the mountain may erode and crumble; the rock that serves as handhold may fall; the climber, a material creature, may stumble, fall, and even die. They can also interact, however, so that the climber makes it to the top and once there experiences a different world. Since it participates in the incarnation, a process of Christogenesis that moves toward the fulfillment of the world and of the climber, the struggle in the world of matter is God's process of bringing consummation. Teilhard is committed to the progress of the world toward God's fulfilling goal. He speaks of "two zones" of matter—that which impedes our progress and threatens to destroy us and that which will bear us to the summit. "The frontier between these two zones is essentially relative and shifting. That which is good, sanctifying and spiritual for my brother below or beside me on the mountainside, can be material, misleading or bad for me."[30] The image of the mountain climber fits the world as a whole. "It would surely not be wrong to suggest that, in its universality, the world too has a prescribed path to follow before attaining its consummation."[31]

Teilhard has composed a kind of prayer to matter that summarizes these themes:

Matter, you in whom I find both seduction and strength …you who can enrich and destroy, I surrender myself to your mighty layers, with faith in the heavenly influences which have sweetened and purified your waters. The virtue of Christ has passed into you. Let your attraction lead me forward, let your sap be the food that nourishes me; let your resistance give me toughness; let your robberies and inroads give me freedom. And, finally, let your whole being lead me towards Godhead.[32]

A Dynamic for Human Activity:
Building the Earth

Although it is a topic of its own, deserving more elaboration than I can do here, it should be noted that Teilhard's celebrated idea of "building the earth" is integral to his view of matter and God's creating work; indeed, it figures in both "My Universe" and *The Divine Milieu*. The material universe in which we are incorporated has produced us as creatures of reflection and action, and this creaturely nature mediates to us the presence of the mystical milieu. At the same time, we contribute to the ongoing creation of the universe and of Christ's body through our activity of creating or building. The process of creative union, bringing the material world to the point of consciousness and spirit, accounts for our emergence as creatures of reflective action. The creation is not finished with us, however. "It continues still more magnificently, and at the highest levels of the world. And we serve to complete it, even by the humblest work of our hands. That is, ultimately, the meaning and value of our acts."[33] Christ is active in every earthly phenomenon, from atom to mystical contemplation. "And in return Christ gains physically from every one of them. Everything that is good in the universe is gathered up by the Incarnate Word as a nourishment that it assimilates, transforms, and divinizes."[34]

"If Christ is omega, nothing is alien to the physical building up of his universal body."[35] Every action, every work, no matter how "humble and unobtrusive," if it is "good"—which means if it aims at supporting the creative union of God—is ultimately directed toward spiritual growth that is fulfilled in Christ.[36] Here we see how the ideas of the mystical milieu and the creating work of God through that milieu become a powerful source of moral and ethical motivation. "Building the earth" has become a familiar way of expressing this ethic, and we know how that can be misunderstood and even perverted. The Christogenic norm and structure of the process provide the necessary content to the idea, and enables us to distinguish between good and evil, between that which serves complexity-consciousness and that which expresses greedy exploitation. We recognize in the spiritual vision, however, that building the earth is not only a moral imperative; it is an ontological and theological necessity. Christogenesis can occur only by passing through the processes of the material.

> Nothing can attain spirit *except along a determined path through matter*. No stage in the journey can be bypassed. Each must be taken in turn; and it would be extremely difficult to say to what depths below us the roots of spirit still extend. The flesh of Christ is fed by the whole universe. The mystical Milieu gathers up everything that is made up of energy. Nothing in the world is completely lacking in power, and nothing is rejected, except that which turns its back on the unification of the spirit.[37]

Summing Up

We return to the eucharistic images with which we began these reflections. Our work, whether scientific or otherwise, and our moral striving in the world do indeed aim at personal fulfillment, material advance, and excellence of performance, but it is the fulfillment, advance, and excellence that are set forth for us in the body and blood of Christ. Our building the earth is not our mastery of the earth, but rather the vehicle of our being consumed by the earth and united with it in processes of complexity. Our building the earth is our pathway into Christogenesis, the fuller becoming of Christ. Christ is the enabler, the God-forward of evolution, and also the criterion of good and evil action.

"If we are worthily to interpret the fundamental place the Eucharist does in fact hold in the economy of the world," we must give attention "to the real, and physical, extensions of the

Eucharistic Presence."[38] The presence of the incarnate Word is in the eucharistic host; it also "attaches itself among us, that is to say in the human zone of the universe," but since Christ is "above all omega," "the universal 'form' of the world," he must be active in "mystically assimilating all that surrounds him"[39]—the entire creation.

Teilhard sums up his vision for the Christian life when he says that the mystical vision discloses both the sacramental consecration of the world by a "complete faith" and communion with the world through a "complete loyalty." Faith focuses on the unification in Christ; loyalty grasps "every opportunity of growing greater and in accepting every summons to die."[40]

Teilhard's is a lofty and stirring mystical vision. Its intellectual and moral scope is vast and formidable. It comes to concrete engagement with all of us individually in the eucharistic imagery and, above all, in the sacramental participation that is its source.

CHAPTER SEVEN

Aspects of Teilhard's Legacy

Nicole Schmitz-Moormann

Fifty years after Teilhard's death, have his life and his thoughts still an impact on today's society? One way to answer this question is to turn to his literary legacy and to look there for topics that moved him and how he reacted to them. Teilhard's literary legacy is vast and I will point out two major aspects in it, namely, the quantitative and qualitative aspects and their respective ramifications.

Addressing the **quantitative legacy** first, it can be said that Teilhard was a very prolific writer. We know about two hundred recipients of *personal and professional letters*. Some correspondence spans several decades, for example: correspondence with George Barbour, Max-Henri Bégouën, Abbé Henri Breuil, P. Pierre Leroy, SJ, P. Henri de Lubac, SJ, Jeanne Mortier, Mgr. Bruno de Solages, Lucile Swan, Ida Treat, P. Auguste Valensin, SJ, Marthe Vaufrey, not to mention his family and relatives, especially Marguerite Teillard Chambon, his cousin.

Between 1940 and 1945, the postal service between China and the rest of the world was almost entirely disrupted, and only on extremely rare occasions was Teilhard offered the opportunity to use the diplomatic bag. His letters give an insight into the actual situation: Only on November 22, 1942, was he told, by an acquaintance in Beijing about the death of his brother Gabriel on October 29, 1941.[1] His geological/paleontological activities were then so seriously restricted that he was thrilled about a possible trip to the close-by Western Hills and Choukoutien. In fact, he and the few people left in Beijing, mostly diplomats, were practically kept prisoners by the Japanese.

> *Pour moi, la guerre a été une période, peut-être féconde, mais complètement monotone. Graduellement, toutes les possibilités de circulation se fermaient, autour de Péking. Et pendant tout ce temps je n'ai pratiquement pas quitté notre petit Institut, toujours dans le même petit cercle de quelques bons amis. J'ai beaucoup publié (très peu a pu encore être distribué),—beaucoup écrit, en marge de la géologie, des Essais peu publiables. Bref, moins les voyages, mon existence a peu changé. Physiquement, je vais toujours bien. Mais vous me retrouvez blanchi..., encore que le coeur soit toujours le même* (UL: Dec. 26, 1945) [For me, war was perhaps a productive, but completely monotonous, period. Gradually all possibilities of traveling around Peking were shut down. During that time I practically did not leave our small institute, and I stay always in the same small circle of some good friends. I published a lot (by now very few papers have been distributed),—I wrote a lot, besides geological matters, some essays which will be hard to publish. In short, travels excepted, my life changed little. Physically, I am still doing fine, but you will see that I have turned gray...but my heart is unchanged.]

Later on, referring to this period, he talked about living in a "fish bowl."

The number of all his *individual writings* are estimated to be above five hundred. They include scientific, philosophical, and theological "Notes, Reports and Essays," "Lectures and Speeches," "Chronicles," "Obituaries," "Prefaces," "Reviews," and "Miscellaneous." His scientific writings, collected and edited in eleven volumes in 1971, revealed the impact of his vast research program both during his lifetime, especially in China, and on science, which is continuing today. In his book *The Story of Peking Man*, Jian Lanpo, the late director of the IVPP[2] in Beijing, emphasized the personal impact of Teilhard's work, updating the Quaternary age in China, and noted:

> The announcement at the meeting of the Zhoukoudian human fossils finds attracted serious attention....There were skeptics though. Among them celebrated scientists like Pierre Teilhard de Chardin. (1990, 27)

Teilhard's so-called *Journal*, handwritten on French school copybooks between July 1915 and April 1955, has 1684 pages (about 3000 typescript pages). The part of it that was written between July 1925 and July 1944 was left behind in China when Teilhard had to leave on a very short notice, abandoning almost all of his books and papers at Peking.

Teilhard's **qualitative** legacy is revealed in his correspondence, his *Journal*, and writings. Teilhard's thoughts and papers have been published in many languages. His famous book *The Human Phenomenon* has been translated into more than thirty languages. Therefore it is important to emphasize the significance of his so-called *Journal* and of his correspondence. For Teilhard his *Journal* was the foremost tool for intellectual reflections. No intimate or emotional outpourings will be found there. Very rarely Teilhard mentions, and only in three or four words, a person, an event, or a crisis without clearly naming them. He wrote down a multitude of ideas and reflections that he developed and deepened over a period of days, of weeks, sometimes of months and even years. Some ideas, partly abandoned, never appeared explicitly in any of his essays. Certain points, only briefly addressed, were not picked up again, although they showed a surprising lucidity about the relevance, importance, or impact of the subject. Other ideas would be revised later and corrected. Still others, elaborated and polished at a certain time or in a certain context, would be integrated later into his vision and then, being very clear to him, would appear in his essays as definitive.

Between November 16, 1924, and May 21, 1925, Teilhard had nine *Journal* entries related to *"Hominisation. Introduction à une étude scientifique du phénomène humain"* [Hominisation. Introduction to a scientific study of the human phenomenon]. On January 2, 1925, he made a first entry about

> *Sujet de Note. Travailler l'hominisation en tant que phénomène tellurique, de premier ordre....*[Subject for a Note. To study hominisation as a first-rate telluric phenomenon....]

and one day later,

> *Plan: Essayer de voir objectivement, dans l'ensemble des choses le phénomène humain.* [Plan: To try to see objectively the human phenomenon throughout the whole of things.]

Were these the first references to what would become, after 1955, his most well-known writing? A first essay on "Phénomène Humain" was finished in September 1928. A second one, to be published in *Revue des questions scientifiques,* was finished in November 1930. We know his intention because we can consult his vast correspondence since his *Journal* is not available between July 1925 and July 1944.

Following Claude Cuénot, I want to emphasize that Teilhard's *correspondence* must already be considered as one of his major works. As in the *Journal,* we can follow the birth and development of ideas, projects, and his different ways of approaching the matter depending on his correspondent. Some examples follow.

About what would become *Le milieu divin,* he wrote to Ida Treat on October 30, 1926 (S-M Coll.):

Il faudra que je vous montre un jour un papier, semi-fiction, que j'ai écrit sur la 'Puissance spirituelle de la Matière', avec une espèce d'hymne à 'Sainte Matière'. [Someday I will have to show you a semi-fictional paper, which I wrote on 'the Spiritual Power of Matter,' with a kind of hymn to 'Holy Matter.']

In a letter dated December 31, 1926 (CC: 1958, 95), we find an early statement about a project to study "Man":

Je conçois de mieux en mieux l'Homme comme le grand phénomène terrestre, celui en lequel culminent les plus grands événements géologiques, et le plus vaste mouvement de la vie. Autrement dit, je découvre des prolongements humains à la Géologic. (CC: 1958, 95) [I better and better see Man as the terrestrial phenomenon, in which the greatest geological events and the widest movement of life peak. In others words, I am discovering human extension in Geology.]

And on January 16, 1927:

J'ai un projet de travail sur l'Homme—non pas l'Homme préhistorique précisément, mais l'Homme regardé comme le plus grand événement tellurique et biologique de notre planète. (CC: 1958, 96) [I have a project on Man—not precisely on prehistoric Man but on Man as the greatest telluric and biological event on our planet.]

Later on, the "evolution" of his project will be the subject of many letters to several friends and colleagues. So on June 28, 1937, he wrote from Murols (Auvergne) to Ida Treat (S-M. Coll.):

...Le livre de ma vie, si j'arrive à le faire, sera simplement intitulé: L'Homme. Encore un ou deux essais préliminaires, et j'essaierai sans doute de l'écrire. [The book of

my life, if I succeed in writing it, will simply be titled *Man*. One or two more preliminary essays, and then I will probably try to write it.]

In a letter to Rhoda de Terra dated June 5, 1938 (L2F: 1968, 122), he shares with her his enthusiasm about his essay on "Man":

> In the meantime, too, I am slowly but steadily preparing my essay on Man, which I will probably start writing this summer. I feel more and more attracted and absorbed by this part of my activity,...I have an impression to perceive more and more distinctively the few central points which, if better understood and conquered, would change the face of our fascinating world.

Between 1938 and 1941, many letters came telling Rhoda about his progress in writing the essay. Considering the contents of letters,[3] the title was definitely changed between 1940 and 1943 to "Le phénomène humain." Then, in a long letter dated March 21, 1941, he reported to Rhoda that the answer he received from Rome two weeks earlier was *"half-and-half."* Teilhard's struggle continued for years. Several times he was asked by censors in Rome to revise the text and then he stated on January 29, 1947:

> ...now it is my turn not to be satisfied with the child... my ideas have developed and improved (I hope) rather much in six years....In fact, I would prefer to write something entirely new....(LTS: 1993, 195)

And on September 2, 1947, he wrote to Rhoda (L2F: 1968, 177):

> ...I should keep quiet (that is to refrain from any publication) for the time being, on the line of philosophy and theology. On scientific matters, no restriction. But where does the limit lie for those people?

Well, I feel quite philosophical about the whole thing, because I know by experience (for the third time, at least) that such handicaps, if well managed, do not stop, but on the contrary help, the progress and diffusion of ideas. (L2F: 1968, 177)

One year later he stated:

I have a feeling that my *Weltanschauung*…is taking rapidly a more definite shape;…and that we become aware of a movement of Mankind as a whole toward increasing arrangement and consciousness (L2F: 1968, 191)

A list of Teilhard's correspondents is, in its diversity, intriguing and fascinating. We see, among others, the name of Davidson Black, a Canadian who started the anatomy department's Cenozoic Era Laboratory at the Peiping Union Medical College; Jeanne Boussac, widow of Jean Boussac of Institut Catholique; Henri Cosme, French minister in China; Christian Dior, mode designer; Madame Georges-Marie Haardt, widow of the explorer Georges-Marie Haardt; Sven Hedin, the explorer; Aldous and Sir Julian Huxley, biologist and first director general of UNESCO; Solange Lemaître, secretary of the World Congress of Faith; Henry de Monfreid, writer, businessman, and explorer, "the pirate"—Teilhard's nickname for him; Roland de Margerie, French ambassador in Peking, Theodore Monod, professor at the Museum; Emmanuel Mounier, personalist philosopher and founder of the well-known review *Esprit*; Kenneth P. Oakley of the Natural History Museum in London; Lucile Swan, a sculptor; Leontine Zanta, the first French woman to receive a PhD in philosophy in Paris in 1914.

There was often considerable variety in a single letter: He could start a letter reporting most technical data and continue on a personal and poetic mood. It is quite significant that Teilhard's letters have been treasured and kept by those to whom he wrote through the years. He did not keep the letters addressed to him but in some cases, thanks to recipients who made carbons of their own letters, we have the back-and-forth of the exchanges.

The contents of "personal letters" addressed to acquaintances, colleagues, and friends reveal his thoughtfulness, his eagerness to listen, his openness to diverse opinions, religions, and races, his apparently endless patience to explain his mind and position, but he was always open and never disguised what he really thought.

> ...[the] idea of a value of sacrifice and pain for the sake of sacrifice and pain itself (whereas the value of pain is simply to pay for some useful conquest!) is a dangerous...perversion of the "meaning of the Cross" (the true meaning of the Cross is: Toward progress through effort). (L2F: 1968, 187)

His letters also reveal his sense of humor:

> *J'ai trouvé là le silence et la tranquillité (malgré beaucoup de puces) dans la propre chambre du Père spirituel (Père Dissard) qui a eu le bon goût d'amasser chez lui, en plus de hardes pour les pauvres, une copieuse collection de romans honnêtes ou peu honnêtes.*[4] (LI: 1972, 125) [I have found there silence and calm (despite plenty of fleas) in the spiritual director's own room (Father Dissard) who has been tactful enough to accumulate, on top of rags for the poor, a good collection of decent, and less decent novels.]

In opposition to the *Journal*, many of his letters to friends and relatives are personal and detailed, revealing his innermost feelings and what moves him. About bouts of depression he wrote to Rhoda:

> For some obscure reasons I do not feel yet exactly myself, physically, or if you prefer, nervously. A mere

accentuation, I guess, of some dispositions which I had to live with since childhood....[5] (L2F: 1968, 134)

About his state of mind on July 5, 1940, he wrote:

...J'en suis à la lettre du 29 mai (Les Eyzies) qui m'a été une douce joie. Mais je voudrais tant savoir ce que vous pensez,—et à quoi ressemble présentement la vie en France,—occupée et non-occupée. Aucune nouvelle de personne, naturellement, depuis la crise....[6] [I got your letter dated May 29 (Les Eyzies) which made me happy. But I would love to know more about what you think,—and how life presently looks like in occupied and non-occupied France. Of course, no news from anybody since the beginning of the crisis.]

To his closest friends he could write about his innermost feelings:

...Je m'en veux d'être si irrégulier dans ma correspondance. Mais je vis toujours dans l'attente de lettres qui ne viennent pas,—et dans l'impression que ce que j'écris n'arrive pas. En fait, jusqu'ici, it semble que vos nouvelles à vous finissent par me parvenir,—avec beaucoup de retard. Mais j'en suis toujours à votre lettre du 22 août. Avec un mot de ma cousine, envoyé du Cantal le 27 août, c'est tout ce que j'ai de plus récent. Ce long silence de partout finit par devenir tout à fait pénible à la longue,—et aussi très déconcertant pour la vie....Cette lettre vous fera sans doute l'effet de venir d'un autre monde, tellement elle doit s'accorder mal avec vos impressions et vos préoccupations du moment. (UL: Nov. 26, 1940) [...I apologize for being so uneven in writing. But, I always live waiting for letters which do not come,—and with the impression that the ones I wrote have not arrived. In fact, until now, it seems that your news ends up

reaching me, although with much delay. Your last letter was dated August 22. With a note from my cousin, sent from Cantal on August 27, they are the most recent ones I got. This long silence from everywhere becomes eventually tiresome, and also very disconcerting in life....This letter will look like it is coming from another world for it will not at all match your actual impressions and pre-occupations.]

Finally, on April 5, 1946, he wrote:

Ces quelques lignes que je "posterai" après-demain à Singapore, pour vous dire que je suis en route, et arriverai à Paris vers le 1r Mai....En tous cas it faudra me prendre tel que je suis,—car je n'ai pas changé, mais plutôt precisé et affirmé mes points de vue depuis 7 ans (!!). Quelle joie ce me sera de vous revoir....—Vous me rajeunirez. (UL) [The day after tomorrow, at Singapore, I will mail to you these few lines to let you know that I am on my way and will arrive Paris about May 1....In any event, you will have to take me as I am, for I have not changed. For the past 7 years I have even more clarified and emphasized my points of view (!!) It will be such a joy seeing you again....—You will make me feel younger.]

The letters open a window on his complex personality full of nuances. They show his immutable moral and religious discipline, as well as the struggles he faced in his intimate, personal, and professional life. He writes spontaneously and he has the gift of telling in all simplicity and sincerity about subjects close to his heart.

While staying with Henri de Monfreid in Somaliland, he wrote to Mme de Monfreid on February 3, 1929 (S-M Coll.):

...Cette existence à deux, dans le "milieu naturel" de Henri, a achevé de me le faire connaître et de nous rapprocher. Je

ne saurais vous dire combien me sont apparus son esprit et son coeur. Vous savez que j'ai eu, et que j'ai beaucoup d'amies. Lui sera un des très rares amis que j'aurai rencontrés. Il me rappelle beaucoup le caractère d'un de mes frères (le meilleur de nous tous peut-être, dans la famille) qui a été tué à la fin de la guerre. [Living together with Henri, in his own natural element, has given me the opportunity to know him in depth and to bring us closer. I could not tell you how much his spirit and his heart became evident to me. You know that I had, and have had, many women friends. Henri is one of the very few male friends I have ever met. He reminds me of the character of one of my brothers (maybe the best among us, in our family) who was killed at the end of the war.]

Next to Henri de Monfreid, other close male friends come to mind: George Barbour, Max-Henri Bégouën, Davidson Black, Henri Breuil, Raymond Jouve, Edouard Le Roy and Pierre Leroy, Auguste Valensin. Claude Cuénot emphasized this aspect of Teilhard's personality in his original unsurpassed biography of Teilhard in French (CC: 1958, 87):

Le P. Teilhard était liant, bien que dans le fond il ne fût accessible qu'à un petit nombre.... [Father Teilhard was sociable, although in depth, he was accessible to few people only....]

He felt as much at ease attending a reception at the Grand Hotel in Beijing as staying with C. C. Young, a Chinese geologist, in a pagoda-turned-school above the Hoang-ho River while on a prospecting trip in 1929. Jia Lanpo, who became in 1938 supervisor of excavation work at Zhoukoudian, wrote (1990, 251):

It was a moving experience to see how many hardships the man could bear. Every time he came to Zhoukoudian, he shared our food and asked for nothing special.

He also recalls Teilhard's personal impact on his and others' works:

When eventually I handed in my twenty-page paper …he went over every sentence, making comments… between almost all the lines….Teilhard spared no effort in educating the young…. (250)

Jia portrays a scene following the tragic death in 1937 of three Chinese workers at Zhoukoudian:

The spontaneous grief he [Teilhard] manifested for his fellow men at that grim moment moved me so much that I can see it in my mind's eye to this day. (251)

Those who met him said that he was at ease with scientists and artists, diplomats, Chinese workers, socialites, religious, atheists, and communists. He recognized and was attracted by original personalities. His antipathies, on the personal level, seem to have been generally reciprocal and rare. Claude Cuénot in his Teilhard biography wrote:

Many different people have testified to the general esteem in which Teilhard was held. His doctor, for example, [was] a Protestant who sometimes discussed with his patient what Teilhard used to call "our little differences of jurisdiction…." (CC: 1958, 298)

His correspondence reveals recurring themes like friendship, love, union, war, peace, humanization, suffering, and so on. It also shows clearly that he was not on a preaching mission. As one example among many, I would like to point to his more than

106

thirty-years correspondence and close friendship with Ida Treat, whom he met at Marcellin Boule's laboratory in Paris in the early '20s and who was the wife of Paul Vaillant-Couturier, a French Communist politician.

Teilhard's letters give us insight into his personality and allow us to follow the development of his projects and thoughts and their application in his personal life. Writing to Rhoda about himself, he stated:

> I have resumed (successfully enough) the writing of my essay on Matter, Love, and Christ. And now I am practically sure to have finished the first of the three main parts before next week. The most difficult part, as I told you, since it deals with the rather intricate roots of my present state of mind. Finally, it turns out to be a piece of psychological analysis rather than an "effusive" or "poetic" description of my youth's experience. (L2F: 1968, 217)

His correspondence with his cousin Marguerite Teillard-Chambon, and with many female friends, allows us to study the meaning and the influence of "le féminin," the feminine, in his own life, as well as his understanding of friendship, love, and chastity. It echoes entries on these topics in the *Journal*. All his friendships with women reflect his thoughts about chastity expressed on May 26, 1918, the day of his final vows:

> ...*Jamais je n'ai mieux compris à quel point l'homme et la femme peuvent se compléter pour s'élever à Dieu.* (CC: 1958, 43) [Never before have I understood better how a man and a woman could complete each other to advance toward God.]

Earlier, on March 12, 1916, he wrote in his *Journal* that

...pour un homme Dieu doit être aimé à travers la femme, en se servant d'elle.... [...for a man, God must be loved through a woman, in using her....]

This statement is so strong, almost disturbing, that we feel the need for complementary explanation. One can be found in an entry dated September 20, 1919:

Pas chercher la femme, mais le Féminin dans toutes les femmes. [Not to seek a woman but the Feminine in all women.]

and on October 4, 1919:

Poursuivre le Féminin dans la femme, sans détruire la femme, et sans s'y laisser enfermer....[To seek after the Feminine in a woman, without destroying her and without being absorbed by her....]

A short sentence in the *Journal* sums his thoughts:

Le luxe du prêtre, c'est d'aimer tout le monde. 15.12.45 [A priest can afford to love everyone.]

One of Teilhard's quests was to seek a personal application for an aspect of energy which he called "love energy":

...I had...the hope that...I could give you a new energy for becoming more yourself, an *energy....And now I realize that I have become for you a center...*—To be an energy, and yet not a center. Is that a mere utopia?... (LTS: 1993, 58)

and few days later:

...if you don't find me as you would, the reason is...the presence of God whom I love as a Person, and to whom I have given the final activity of my life....You, you are searching an equilibrium "à deux"; and for me, this is a question "à trois." (LTS: 1990, 59)

In a letter dated August 14, 1950, Teilhard tells Rhoda about his recent project *Le coeur de la matière* (CM) and writes:

> ...the *Féminin* will be presented and discussed as a kind of Conclusion or *Envoi*: not so much as an element by itself than as a light illuminating the whole process of concentration: *really*, as I wrote to you, "the spirit of Union."

In the *Journal* numerous entries are related to "union" and its different aspects. The subject is among those most often reflected upon by Teilhard. So on April 8, 1919:

> *Distinguer les 3 unions organiques:*
>   *1) union de rivalité: les éléments, en luttant les uns contre les autres, créent un équilibre progressif (à la limite inférieur = union d'inertie)*
>   *2) union d'utilité (économique et égoiste) (cf. polypiers): adaptation mutuelle par "Taylorisme,"[7] avantages réciproques.*
>   *3) union dans l'âme et la vie (= transformation des précédents) = les elements s'unissent*

> [3 types of organic union to be distinguished:
>   1) union of rivalry: elements, while fighting each other, create a gradual equilibrium (union of inertia at the inferior limit)
>   2) union of utility (economical and selfish [motivation]) (cf. coral): mutual adaptation by "Taylorism," reciprocal advantages
>   3) Union in soul and life (= transformation of 1) and 2)) = elements unite]

Later, on May 20, 1950:

1) *eu-union*, union of identification: love from center to center. (Union is essentially effect of Love—God is All in all—St Paul)
2) fusion, identification (Attitude without love—God is All)
3) mechanization (identical with union of dissolution?)

On September 7, 1953:

LA différence Est/Ouest: pour l'Est (Inde), quoiqu'il fasse, l'union fait disparaître l'Ego. Pour l'Ouest, elle l'accentue. [toujours la confusion entre individu et personne = ego] [THE difference between East and West: for the East (India), whatever the *Ego* does, union makes it disappear. For the West, union emphasizes the Ego. [always the confusion between individual and person = ego]

The very title of an essay written in September 1917 is something of a shock: "*La nostalgie du front.*" At first, the choice of the word *nostalgie* is difficult to understand coming from a priest, a Jesuit, who lost two brothers during World War I, who was on the front line at Douaumont, Verdun, and Chemin des Dames, who won a number of citations, the Croix de Guerre and Médaille Militaire. Answers can be found in his *Journal* and letters. The front gave him a unique experience. Refusing to work as a chaplain behind the lines, he served as a stretcher bearer in a Moroccan regiment and lived daily life with men who came from various social origins, intellectual backgrounds, and beliefs. For the first time in his life he was immersed in a multiethnic, complex world and soon, seeing beyond the visible, he perceived the spiritual potential that held humanity together. On December 11, 1939, writing from Beijing to his brother Joseph, his reflections evaluate the new conflict and recall his state of mind during World War I (LV: 1956, 244):

...ce sera une autre forme de guerre, dans les esprits et dans les coeurs. Le danger, de rester, est que je risque de me décrocher du mouvement humain vrai, comme ceux qui n'ont pas connu le front en 1914–1918. [...this one will be another form of war, in people's minds and hearts. The danger in staying here, is that I risk to get off the *real* human movement, like those who did not know the front during 1914–1918.]

Also in a letter to P. Leroy, dated January 1, 1951, he writes:

J'ai naturellement horreur de la guerre (que je considère comme un régime destiné à disparaître un jour,—sous sa forme d'entre-tuement)...les hommes ne feront plus rien de bon tant qu'ils n'auront pas pris conscience du mouvement (organique) qui les entraîne, et qu'ils doivent aider, et cette conscience ne leur viendra que par une série de bonnes secousses.... (LPL: 1976, 90) [I naturally hate war (which I consider a system that, under its form of killing, will someday disappear)...humans will do nothing right as long as they will not become aware of the organic movement that pulls them, and which they must help, and this awareness will only come to them after a series of major shocks....]

On the subject of politics, war, and peace, Teilhard's letters to Rhoda de Terra are also explicit. On October 6, 1939, he wrote to her:

...I do not react to the crisis as I did in 1914. Even I have the suspicion that in Europe, in spite of being decided to bring the Nazis down, people do *not* have any *spirit* of war. Would it be possible that we are gradually getting *"vaccinated"* against spells of mere brutal violence?...But

I have a kind of feeling that we are going toward tremendous political and social changes through an *abortive* war. And by the changes only I am interested. When they come out, an internationalist (and really "Earthy") objective and ideal will be required. Along this line of research I can perhaps do something. (L2F: 1968, 135)

On December 13, 1939:

And still I cannot yet be really excited by this war....I have an obscure feeling that the Allies are fighting too much for quietness and stability (or rather immobility); and this point becomes always clearer in myself; the only fight in which I would like to mix and to die should be a battle for construction and movement ahead...[there are] two different types of crusaders and martyrs: those who were killed for keeping, and those who were killed for changing, an old thing. (L2F: 1968, 138)

On June 18, 1940, again to Rhoda:

My hope is that, from awakening to the threat of a mechanized Earth, we shall be forced into the conception of and the belief in a spiritual structure of the world....This is the very moment, paradoxically, for Man to discover the biological value, and the possible extension, of the only energy which can group and achieve individual Man, without turning him into a gadget or slave: a mutual form of love, based on the consciousness of a common Something (or rather Somebody) into which all together we converge. (L2F: 1968, 145)

And on August 3, 1940:

But did [France and England] not precisely make a mistake on the true meaning of "peace"? "Peace" cannot mean anything but a *higher process of conquest*. And, since 1919, France at least did scarcely do more than to stick comfortably to the old routines. The World is bound to belong to its most active elements. (L2F: 1968, 146)

While considering his views on war, it is interesting to see how he applied the words *statics* and *dynamics* to this topic:

Distinguer paix statique et paix dynamique. [We have to distinguish between static peace and dynamic peace.] (*Journal*, April 5, 1945)

One explanation of these words is found in a letter to Max and Simone Bégouën written on September 20, 1940:

L'époque de la guerre est passée, comme celle de la paix conçue comme un repos. La paix n'est pas le contraire de la guerre. Elle est la guerre portée au-delà et plus haut qu'elle-même, dans la conquête du transhumain (cette montée dépend des volontés humaines harmonisées dans un effort commun). (LV: 1956, 260) [The age of war is gone, like that of peace conceived as a repose. Peace is not the opposite of war. It is war carried beyond and above itself in the conquest of the transhuman (this ascent depends on human wills harmonized into a common effort).]

Also on October 14, 1940:

Plus le monde est en crise, plus il faut chercher à développer un effort constructif, qui absorbe, dans la véritable paix (càd. dans un super-effort en commun) l'esprit de la guerre....(UL) [The more the world goes through a crisis, the more we must try to develop a constructive effort, which will absorb the spirit of war into a true peace.]

And on November 26, 1940:

Je crois, de tout mon coeur, que quelque chose tend à se reconstituer et à renaître là-bas,—et je voudrais m'y consacrer. En tous cas il me paraît difficile (et il serait dangeureux qu'elle se termine) sans de profonds ré-ajustements du monde, et sans le triomphe d'une "mystique". Il ne servirait à rien de fixer un ordre nouveau par "compulsion" ou "coercition".... (UL) [I believe, with all my heart, that, over there, something strives to re-form and to come back to life, and I would like to devote myself to it. In any event it seems to me difficult (and it would be dangerous that the war ends) without any deep readjustment of the world, and without the triumph of some "mystics." It would not do any good to fix a new order by way of "compulsion" or "coercion"....]

On January 20, 1941, to his brother Joseph Teilhard:

Il n'y aura je crois de vraie paix que lorsque les hommes se seront entendus, au moins en première approximation, sur ce que nous devons attendre et espérer d'un avenir de la Terre. (LV: 1956, 270) [There will be no real peace, I believe, until men will agree, at least on a first approximation, about what we should expect and hope for from the world's future.]

And on June 22, 1941, to Rhoda:

Nothing can save us except the awakening of Man to interhuman affinities. Biologically and physically, the thing is overwhelming *evident*. The difficulty is to find the match which will light the fire. (L2F: 1968, 158)

Over the years he considered such questions as love and the feminine, peace and war, mystics[8] and science, matter and spirit,

114

statics and dynamics, planetization and omegalization, unity and union, and so on. As with the words *statics* and *dynamics*, Teilhard uses the word *mystics* in various contexts, like war (see UL above), religion, sciences, and so on.

On April 28, 1945, he wrote in his *Journal*:

En fait, mystique Chinoise (unification avec le Monde civil, astral et céleste) correspond à une mystique occidentale statique.... [In fact, Chinese mystics, (unification with the civil, astral and celestial World) corresponds to a static occidental mystics]

The words *mystics* and *science* appear often side by side:

Les vrais moines d'aujourd'hui: les chercheurs. (12.5.1950) [The real monks of today are the researchers.]

He sees even his personal mysticism in the light of evolution. On February 1945, he notes:

La Mystique = un contact évolutif avec Dieu [Mystics = an evolutionary contact with God]

And on May 7, 1948:

Toute ma Mystique: la force ascensionnelle du Christ,— augmentée et 'attelée' à l'Evolution [My whole mystic (is) the upward force of Christ,—increased by, and "harnessed" to Evolution].

This explains what he wrote on July 25, 1944, namely:

Mystique de l'Évolution = Mystique de la Recherche [Mystics of evolution = Mystics of research]

An excerpt from a letter to Rhoda resumes his attitude toward Eastern mystics:

[E.M. and I] had a long talk on Vedant mystics, which I distrust more and more (because I think that it solves incorrectly and even sophistically the fundamental problem of Unity, and logically destroys Love).

Many letters revealed how he viewed himself and his work. Here a short selection follows: About himself, he wrote on May 12, 1936, to Lucile Swan:

I am not a preacher…but a desperate searcher (LTS: 1993, 59)

To Jeanne Mortier, on April 7, 1950:

Je suis un enfant de la Terre 'avant' d'être un homme de Dieu! 'Avant' en ce sens que, irrémédiablement, par structure intime, je ne puis saisir le Divin qu'à travers le cosmique…vous ne me comprendrez jamais si vous ne voyez pas cela. (SM Coll.) [I am a child of the Earth "before" being a man of God! "before" in the sense that, irremediably, by intimate structure, I only can grasp the Divine through the Cosmic….If you do not see that, you will never understand me.]

On April 13, 1940:

(…) *plus les années passent, plus je commence à croire que ma fonction, aura simplement été d'être, à l'image bien réduite du Baptiste, celui qui annonçait et appelait ce qui devait venir.* (S-M Coll.) [The more the years go by, the more I begin to think that my role has simply been, just like the Baptist, but on a much smaller scale, to be one who announces and calls for what is to come.]

This echoes decades of old entries in his *Journal* where his state of mind can be studied. He wrote on March 5, 1919:

Je veux continuer à faire des Sciences—pour influencer les autres et pour vivre personnellement la transition du K(osmos) in X(rist). [I will continue to do Sciences...so to influence others and to live personally the transition of K(osmos) into X(rist).]

And on August 20, 1921:

Accord certain entre Foi et Science: à condition que les deux convergent....La Science ne viendra pas aux pieds du Théologien. [An accord between Faith and Sciences is certain, provided both converge. Science will not come to the feet of the Theologian.]

On October 26, 1948:

instinctivement et contre mes principes, j'aime la Nature plus que l'Homme. Je n'aime l'Homme qu'à titre de phénomène naturel (cosmique) en l'intégrant dans la Nature. [instinctively and against my principles I love Nature more than Man. I love Man only as natural (cosmic) phenomenon, as an integrated part of Nature.]

This echoes an entry dated August 19, 1944:

La Science mène au Divin,—est un accès moderne au Divin.... [Science leads to the Divine, it is a modern access to the Divine....]

For decades, Teilhard's name has been linked with the idea of globalization. I have searched his journals for this topic. He did not write extensively about "globalization" ("mondialisme" in

French) but about "planetization" and November 21, 1945, he wrote in his *Journal* of a

distinction between noogenesis and planetization.

He continued:

> ...*planétisation* = *une phase dans noogénèse...elle a commencé avec Hominisation, elle est la phase terminale de Noogénèse.* [planetization is a phase of hominization in noogenesis. Planetization has begun with Hominization and it is the final phase of noogenesis.]

Between 1945 and 1950 he emphasizes the spiritual function of planetization. On September 2, 1950, he noted:

> *un lien cosmique entre Planétisation (et) Christification.* [there is a cosmic link between planetization and christification.]

Planetization is the final phase of noogenesis, and a phase toward omegalization. and on September 10, 1950, he made it clear:

> *Aussi vain de se rebiffer devant la Planétisation humaine que devant le mouvement des astres, l'Énergie nucléaire.* [It is as vain to rebel against human planetization as against the movement of the planets and against nuclear energy.]

A distinctive aspect of Teilhard's legacy is his vocabulary. Very early, he realized that traditional language was not able, at least partially, to convey his thoughts. He developed multiple neologisms like *spirit-matter, complexity-consciousness, radial and tangential energy, noosphere, omegalization,* and so on.

He was aware of the necessity to define his vocabulary. On March 20, 1955, he planned, but never finished, *"some kind of 'lexikon' explaining my terms."*

Teilhard's intellectual legacy can also be found throughout his published works. An extremely brief summary of his thoughts can be read in a 1948 article that he wrote about himself to be published. Titled *"Ma position intellectuelle"* ("My intellectual position"), the first sentence reads "Essentially P. Teilhard de Chardin's thinking is not expressed in some metaphysics, but in some kind of phenomenology"...and in his own words, from an entry dated June 25, 1952:

Mes grandes illluminations:

1) L'Union différencie (personnalise, Péking 1937)

2) Compléxité "engendre" la Conscience (Péking, 1942)

3) La Réflexion croît

4) La Convergence de l'Univers

5) L'Evolution converge

ou plus tard:

Le Kosmos converge

La Convergence réfléchit

Réflexion christifie

My great insights:

1) Union differentiates (personalizes, Peking 1937)

2) Complexity "engenders" consciousness (Peking 1942)

3) Reflection increases

4) Convergence of the Universe

5) Evolution converges

or later:

Kosmos converges

Convergence reflects

reflection christifies

Teilhard's legacy is reflected best in his personal prayer to Christ:

> *Seigneur, parce que tout l'instinct et par toutes les chances de ma vie, je n'ai jamais cessé de vous chercher et de vous placer au coeur de la matière universelle, c'est dans l'éblouissement d'une universelle transparence et d'un universel embrasement que j'aurai la joie de fermer les yeux.* (CC: 1958, 469) [Lord, since with every instinct of my being and through all the changing fortunes of my life, it is you whom I have ever sought, you whom I have set at the heart of universal matter, it will be in a resplendence which shines through all things and in which all things are ablaze, that I shall have the felicity of closing my eyes.]

Conclusion

Teilhard's literary legacy may be described quantitatively and qualitatively. He was a prolific letter writer to both personal and professional friends. In addition to the eleven published volumes of his scientific writings, his personal *Journal* remains the foremost tool for understanding his intellectual reflections. Hopefully, this review of some of the principal themes that appear in his correspondence and in his *Journal* will increase appreciation for the remarkable insights of Teilhard de Chardin.

References

CM   *Le coeur de la matière*, Oeuvres, Ed. du Seuil, Paris, 1955–76.

LF   *Lettres familières de Pierre Teilhard de Chardin mon ami.* Pierre Leroy, SJ, Ed. du Centurion, 1976.

L2F   *Letters to Two Friends.* The New American Library. New York, NY, 1968.

LI	*Lettres intimes à Auguste Valensin, Bruno de Solages, Henri de Lubac.* Paris, Aubier-Montaigne, 1972.
LTS	*The Letters of Teilhard de Chardin and Lucile Swan.* Georgetown Univ. Press, 1993.
LV	*Lettres de voyages (1923–1955).* Paris, Grasset, 1956.
MD	*Le milieu divin.* Paris, Le Seuil, 1957.
NF	*La nostalgie du front.* In *Ecrits du temps de la guerre.* Paris, Grasset, 1965.
OSc.	*L'oeuvre scientifique.* Ed. and comp. Nicole Schmitz-Moormann and Karl Schmitz-Moormann. Preface by Jean Piveteau. 11 vols. Olten, Walter Verlag, 1971.
PH	*Le phénomène humain.* Ed. Jeanne Mortier. Paris, Le Seuil, 1955.
SM Coll.	Schmitz-Moormann Collection. Woodstock Theological Center Library. Washington, D.C.
UL	Unpublished letters.

Claude Cuénot. 1958. *Pierre Teilhard de Chardin. Les grandes étapes de sa vie.* Paris, Plon.
Jian Lanpo and Huang Weiwen. 1990. *"The story of Peking Man" from Archaeology to Mystery.* Beijing Foreign Languages Press, Hong-Kong, and Oxford University Press, Oxford.

CHAPTER EIGHT

Pierre Teilhard de Chardin: Priest, Scientist, and Mystic

James W. Skehan, SJ

"There is a communion with God, and a communion with earth, and a communion with God through earth."
Teilhard, 1916; 1965:14

A Perspective on Teilhard's Life and Writings

Over fifty years have passed since Teilhard de Chardin's death on Easter Sunday, April 10, 1955. Teilhard died one month short of his seventy-fifth birthday, having been born on May 1, 1881, in the Province of Auvergne, in central France. Teilhard, as he was generally known, was a highly educated Jesuit geologist-paleontologist who, because of his scientific background concerned with origins, was deeply concerned that the Catholic Church at the time did not "see" the important implications inherent in the "new eucharistic theology" joined to a wide-ranging creation theology.

Although Teilhard was forbidden by the Vatican's Holy Office to publish his writings on spirituality during his lifetime, his manuscripts and other writings have fortunately been preserved and have been largely published and today enjoy worldwide acclaim. Since his death, his thought and spirituality have become better known and understood because timely commentaries by scholars have been published on a wider spectrum of disciplines than could have been imagined fifty years ago.

At the same time, Teilhard's voluminous scientific research on regional geology and human paleontology, in China and elsewhere, was accessible in French geoscience journals and in publications of the Geological Survey of China, among others. Although Teilhard's scientific publications were of no concern to the Vatican's Holy Office, they also have been preserved and reprinted. These have been published in well-known geoscience journals including the *Bulletin of the Geological Society of France*, publications of the Geological Survey of China, and others. Several years after his arrival in Peking, Teilhard was invited in 1929 to serve as advisor to the director of the Geological Survey of China. Additionally, Teilhard served as a working scientist to help plan and carry out geological and paleontological research over the vast reaches of China.

Teilhard's Career Turns to China

Having completed four years of military service (1914–1919), a brilliant PhD thesis, and having been appointed to the prestigious chair of geology in the Institut Catholique in Paris, left vacant by the death of Professor Boussac, it was expected that Teilhard would "inevitably rise to the upper echelons in French academic circles." However, that prospect was short-circuited because he was required by his religious superiors in Rome to leave his academic position in Paris and go into exile from France. This turn of events came about because of serious misunderstandings concerning questions raised in ecclesiastical circles concerning Teilhard's orthodoxy regarding certain Catholic doctrines such as original sin (Skehan, 2001; Lukas and Lukas, 1981).

Accordingly, Teilhard, with the approval of his religious superiors in France, set out for China and in the process began a long exile in China in the early 1920s. Initially, Teilhard was sent by the Paris Museum in 1923 to participate in a scientific expedition along the Yellow River in China. That four-month expedition was so fruitful that Teilhard extended his stay so that he could make another expedition into the high Mongolian plateau and the Gobi Desert in 1924. Between expeditions he visited Peking where he met American anthropologists, geologists, and paleontologists.

A new world was opening for Teilhard because he saw geology in a much broader perspective than previously. Additionally, he correctly forecast certain directions in which the science would develop in succeeding decades. Although Teilhard was aware of theories of continental drift, data critical for the developing theories of large-scale plate tectonic movements of the Earth's crust were yet to be discovered, in large part by the kinds of research in geophysics that Teilhard had envisioned. The expeditions that Teilhard undertook in China and his contacts with Chinese colleagues and other foreign nationals working in China expanded his geological and paleontological horizons.

Eastern Asia had become attractive for the significant research opportunities that it appeared to offer. The decades between his first expeditions in China and his departure in 1946 were scientifically Teilhard's most fruitful period. In addition Teilhard received several significant honors, including the Mendel Medal awarded by Villanova University in 1937 and induction into the Academy of Sciences of France. These were signs of a growing recognition that with time he was nearing the highest level of academic achievement. Besides, Teilhard made time to write on topics of science and religion and especially to rethink and expand his ideas and subject matter of interest that he had explored earlier in his career (Skehan, 2001).

In his more than thirty years as a research scientist, Teilhard had published the voluminous results of his scientific research. Predictably, during Teilhard's lifetime these publications on evolution and human activities in eastern Asia were of great interest to scientists of the international community who were aware of the relevance of his research to their own work. This was especially the case of writings by Teilhard and his colleagues of the China Geological Survey who published the results of the discovery and description of *Sinanthropus pekinensis*, better known to the general public as *Peking man*. These scientists were primarily geologists, paleontologists, and anthropologists working in eastern and southeastern Asia, but others working in Africa and Europe as well. In addition, Teilhard's work fitted nicely into the Scientific Mission of the Jesuits, who maintained a tradition of corporate scientific research that had flourished in China since it was begun by the Jesuit Matteo Ricci. He was the first of a number of distinguished Jesuit scientists who were admitted into China from 1582 until 1947 (Skehan, 2001).

Perspectives on Teilhard's Orthodoxy

Teilhard's manuscripts and essays on religion, as well as his scientific publications, numbering some five hundred items, were first published in French or remained unpublished at the time of his death in 1955. Teilhard's writings on religious topics were preserved by dedicated friends and eventually published. Even after his writings were translated into English in the late 1950s and 1960s, it took a long time for them to be accepted by theologians and philosophers because Teilhard's thought was expressed commonly in terms that he invented or that were unconventional. Thus it took many years for scholars, theologians, and biographers to examine his thought and writings before coming to a fully sympathetic appreciation of them.

Teilhard's religious superiors commissioned a noted French Jesuit theologian and cardinal, Henri de Lubac, to evaluate the orthodoxy of his writings, which he did in 1965 in two books, *Teilhard de Chardin: The Man and His Meaning*, 1965, and *The Religion of Teilhard de Chardin*, 1968. Because Cardinal de Lubac had been appointed by Pope John XXIII as one of two Vatican representatives to draw up the agenda for the Vatican Council of the early 1960s, and because of the high degree of credibility that he enjoyed as a result of his evaluation of Teilhard's orthodoxy, the cloud of suspicion hovering over Teilhard appeared progressively less ominous. "Over the approximately one-half century since Teilhard's death his writings have been recognized as very exciting Christocentric extensions and interpretations of traditional Catholic teaching" (Skehan, 2001:19).

Henri de Lubac (1965) makes the important point that the person of Christ was "the dominant influence upon the elaboration of what Teilhard termed in English his 'personalistic universe.' Personalism is indeed at the heart of his system" (p. 22), leading him ultimately to conclude:

> the Christ of revelation is quite simply Omega. To demonstrate this fundamental proposition, I need only to refer to the long series of Johannine and especially Pauline texts where the physical supremacy of Christ over the universe is affirmed in terms which are magnificent....There we have the very definition of Omega. (p. 89)

They all come down to these two essential affirmations of cosmic importance that Teilhard accepted quite literally:

> "He is before all things" (Col. 1:17) and "the head of every principality and power" (Col. 2:10) so that Christ is all in all (Col. 3:11).
>
> Ordinarily we cannot see the air we breathe, but our life depends on it at all times. God, like the air, "encompasses us on all sides, like the world itself. The only thing that prevents us from enfolding him in our arms is our "inability to see him." (*Divine Milieu*, 1960:46)

Pope John Paul II—*Gift and Mystery*

In celebrating the fiftieth anniversary of his own priesthood in 1995, Pope John Paul II wrote the book *Gift and Mystery*. In it His Holiness used a text from Teilhard's "Mass" to convey what the Mass meant to him: The Eucharist is "celebrated in order to offer 'on the altar of the whole earth the world's work and suffering,'" using, as he pointed out, the beautiful words of Teilhard de Chardin.

Pope John Paul II—*Encyclical, 2003*

Pope John Paul II celebrates another doctrinal milestone in eucharistic theology in his encyclical, *Ecclesia de Eucharistia*, April 17, 2003, in which he remembers fondly the many chapels and cathedrals in which these eucharistic celebrations in which he participated took place. He summed up his experience with a word, *cosmic*, that surely echoed Teilhard's "Mass on the World." "This varied scenario of celebrations of the eucharist has given me a powerful experience of its universal and, so to speak cosmic character. Yes, Cosmic! Because even when it is celebrated on the humble altar of a country church, the eucharist is always in some way celebrated on the altar of the world. It unites heaven and earth. It embraces and permeates all creation...this is the *mysterium fidei* which is accomplished in the eucharist. The world which came forth from the hands of God the Creator now returns to him redeemed by Christ" (*Origins*, v. 32: no. 46, May 1, 2003).

Joseph Cardinal Ratzinger—*Spirit of the Liturgy*

In Joseph Cardinal Ratzinger's book, *Spirit of the Liturgy* (2000: 29), the present Holy Father, Pope Benedict XVI, wrote about the goal of worship and creation. He states that "as a whole both worship and creation are one and the same—divinization, a world of freedom and love. But this means that the historical makes its appearance in the cosmic…against the background of the modern evolutionary world view, Teilhard de Chardin depicted the cosmos as a process of ascent, a series of unions…leading to the 'Noosphere'.…Invoking the epistles to the Ephesians and Colossians, Teilhard looks on Christ as the energy that strives toward the Noosphere and finally incorporates everything in its 'fullness.' …From here Teilhard went on to give new meaning to Christian worship: the transubstantiated Host is the anticipation of the transformation and divinization of matter in the Christological 'fullness.' In his view, the Eucharist provides the movement of the cosmos with its direction; it anticipates its goal and at the same time urges it on" (Ratzinger, 2000: 28–29).

Geologist and Paleontologist

Over the years I have developed a growing interest in Teilhard, the Jesuit research geologist and paleontologist, and over the past thirty-five years, also in Teilhard the mystic. While I was a young Jesuit I approached Teilhard's writings on spirituality guardedly, attempting to sort out whether I, as a future Jesuit professor of geology, might encounter the same kind of problems and treatment from the Holy Office as Teilhard had because of writings on spirituality. Since his death there has appeared an extraordinarily large volume of Teilhard's writings on spirituality and personal correspondence. A rarely spoken concern that seems to have hovered around Teilhard is the question: If he were a first-rate geoscientist, how was it possible for Teilhard to find the time and energy for high-quality publications in the geosciences as well as in spirituality?

The intense enthusiasm on the part of scholars and others for Teilhard's writings on spirituality has grown exponentially. A substantial number of scholars in theology, including mystical theology, have praised Teilhard's writings, including notably the

Jesuit theologian Harvey Egan (1982, 77–97) in *What Are They Saying About Mysticism*. The Jesuit theologian Thomas M. King (1981) has written about Teilhard the mystic in *Teilhard's Mysticism of Knowing*. Ursula King has written several excellent books, also on Teilhard the mystic, 1980, 1996, 1997, and 2002.

However, I have been intensely interested over the years in evaluating the scientific stature of Teilhard the geologist. The following are my reflections on some contrasts between the visible productivity of scholars in the observational sciences and those concerned with spirituality and mysticism. My own experience of the time-consuming demands required to carry out geological research in the field, laboratory, library, and for publication in scientific journals and books may be relevant. I have a growing and firm conviction that Teilhard must be regarded as a towering giant for his prodigious record of publication in both the geological sciences and in spirituality.

Spiritual Exercises: Jesuit Spirituality

Since Teilhard's death he has been honored in part for his works on spirituality and especially for his writings on mystical theology. Such writing by well-educated Jesuits is appropriate because it is in the mainstream of Jesuit tradition even for Jesuit scientists. That this should be so is appropriate since Ignatius, founder of the Society of Jesus (commonly referred to as the Jesuit order) was himself one of the great mystics in the Roman Catholic tradition. The personal transformation of Ignatius from a life of dissipation while soldiering as a young man is chronicled in the little book of personal and religious reflections that Ignatius called *Spiritual Exercises* as well as in other autobiographical writings and letters. The personal and religious transformation of Ignatius and of those whose spiritual motivation is solidly grounded on these Christ-centered *Spiritual Exercises* represents a remarkable legacy of spirituality, including a tradition of mysticism.

A fundamental aspect of Ignatian spirituality consists in "finding God in all things" because that perspective is the driving force that provides the motivation inherent in fidelity to the *Spiritual Exercises*. The history of the Jesuit order and Ignatius's statements of purpose make it clear that a primary way for his followers to serve in uplifting the culture is by means of education. The concept of "finding God in all things" is a motivational concept for creatively coming to envision how Ignatius's followers might choose as a course of action "the greater good" rather than being content to just "do good."

A way of visualizing the spirituality embodied in the *Spiritual Exercises* is that they consist of the ideal of living the "three dimensional" work, so to speak, of attending both to "the Ahead" as well as "the Above." "The Ahead" refers to every aspect of human progress in which we may participate, such as scientific teaching or research, and "the Above" consists of "finding God" in all aspects of the work and in every aspect of life as lived. Unlike the passive mysticism of the Middle Ages, Teilhard's is an Ignatian mysticism of union with God through action. Ursula King in these insightful books on mysticism (1980, 1996, and 1997) has written extensively about Teilhard's new mysticism.

Teilhard presents an important perspective on his "new mysticism" that he sums up as "a communion with God through action":

> How can we, following the call of St. Paul, see God in all the active half of our lives? In fact, through the unceasing operation of the Incarnation, the divine so thoroughly permeates all our creaturely energies that, in order to meet it and lay hold on it, we could not find a more fitting setting, that of our action.
>
> To begin with, in action I adhere to the creative power of God, I coincide with it. I become not only its

instrument but its living extension. And, as there is nothing more personal in a being than his will, I merge myself in a sense, through my heart, with the very heart of God. (Teilhard 1960: 62–63)

A 450-year-old Jesuit Tradition

Ignatius of Loyola, with like-minded companions educated at the University of Paris, founded the Jesuit order in 1540. Although Ignatius was no scientist, he recognized from the beginning the need for the order to include men highly educated in various fields of human endeavor. The early Jesuits undertook activities where they perceived the needs were urgent, many of which involved teaching; and often enough they were called "geometers," that is, teachers of pre-calculus mathematics and science that they applied to astronomy. As early as 1582 Matteo Ricci, a former student of fellow Jesuit mathematician Christopher Clavius, was permitted entrance into China. In time his reputation as mathematician and astronomer brought him to the attention of the emperor. As a result he was asked to serve as Imperial Astronomer and was elevated to the rank of Mandarin. His skills paved the way for two younger Jesuits to succeed him as Imperial Astronomers, and to receive permission to speak publicly of the Christian religion.

Ricci's success has been attributed "to his personal qualities, his complete adaptation to Chinese customs and to his authoritative knowledge of the sciences" (MacDonnell, 1989). This was an auspicious beginning of the long history of Jesuits working in scientific research and religious teaching in China and around the world.

The Need for a New Mysticism

To understand why Teilhard had a lifelong preoccupation with human evolution it is necessary to think of it not only as a scientific question linked to his background as a geologist-paleontologist. In addition, with a keen pastoral sense, Teilhard recognized through-out his adult life the unfulfilled spiritual hunger of many of his fel-low Christians who felt separated simultaneously from a total dedication both to "building their world" and from a heartfelt "communion with God." He expressed his recognition of this need as follows:

> We need a new theology and a new approach to per-fection...to meet the new needs and aspirations....But what we need perhaps even more...is for a new and higher form of worship to be gradually disclosed by Christian thought and prayer, adapted to the needs of tomorrow's believers without exception. (Teilhard de Chardin, 1988; cited by U. King, 1997:2; and Skehan, 2005:13)

Thomas King (1988), a Jesuit theologian and Teilhardian scholar, holds that, by contrast with some other spiritual writers, Teilhard claims that "one is able to ascend (to God) by uniting one-self with the material world. For Teilhard, the material world con-tains the power we need for the ascent to God. So for Teilhard the basis for any form of mysticism required that one begin with the Cosmic Sense" (T. King, 1988:64). In short, this is what Teilhard regarded as a "new mysticism" (Skehan, 2005). The "Cosmic Sense" that Teilhard spoke of so often resonates with what Pope John Paul II referred to in his encyclical, *Ecclesia de Eucharistia*, as "a powerful experience of the universal," a linking of the actual celebration of the Eucharist "on the humble altar of a country church" to the Eucharist that is always in some way celebrated on the altar of the world, thus framing this experience in a mystical context.

The characteristics of Teilhard's dynamic personality and the factors that shaped Teilhard's influential life and scientific career led him to recognize the need for a new mysticism. The core of Teilhard's approach to a new mysticism or spirituality has been summed up in several of his phrases, "building the Earth" and "communion with God through Earth." A part of what Teilhard seems to have understood by those phrases "was the urgent need for Christianity to become more in tune with the culture and spirit of the times. He felt that the harmony that he recognized between the Pauline and Johannine biblical texts and evolution could help Christians and non-Christians to develop a similar harmonious understanding of how they might go about building the earth" (Skehan, 2005:13).

Teilhard: Fashioned by Spirituality and Science

Childhood family influences left a profound stamp on the geologist-paleontologist and on the Jesuit priest that Teilhard became. His father, Emmanuel, a student of natural history, fostered an interest in neighboring volcanic mountains in the Auvergne region of the Massif Central of France. His mother, Berthe-Adele de Dompierre d'Hornoy, was a devout Catholic whose spiritual reading included writings of the medieval mystics, and whose spirituality was strongly focused on devotion to the Sacred Heart of Jesus. Teilhard said of his mother at the time of her death, "To her I owe the best part of my soul." Teilhard was enrolled in the Jesuit school in Villefranche-sur-Saône and in 1899 became a novice in the Jesuit novitiate in Aix-en-Provence.

From his earliest days as a young Jesuit in studies, Teilhard had a consuming interest in geology. He was concerned with evolution not only as a significant biological concept and process but also as having religious significance. Teilhard's life's goal revolved around the christological problem of rethinking "the total mystery of Christ in terms of 'genesis' or 'becoming.'" Teilhard's geological and paleontological studies enhanced his conviction that he lived in a dynamic universe (Mooney, 1964:62). Teilhard was concerned with two problems: In light of the incarnation, "what is the relationship between Jesus of Nazareth and evolution? And what is the relationship of the cosmos to the same Jesus," the second person of the divine Trinity? As a result Teilhard's writings on evolution have taken on great significance in light of his theology of the incarnation and creation. Teilhard enjoyed the theological richness of humans participating in what may be referred to as "ongoing creation" which he also termed "building the Earth."

During the formative years of his life of scholarship and spirituality, Teilhard began to formulate some of his important mystical concepts. One of these links was the cosmic significance of Christ's life, death, and resurrection to the cosmic evolution of life itself, for which Jesus as the Creator of the universe is responsible. In Teilhard's view the *Parousia* represents the final culmination of God's plan of salvation for the human race and as such corresponds to Teilhard's initial understanding of Omega as the totality of earth's collective reflection at the end of time.

Fundamentally Teilhard accepted the term *Omega* in scripture as referring to "the supreme personal Being here and now responsible for the time process itself, the real Omega, the Prime Mover ahead who not only is but has always been." Teilhard's assumption was that if the Christ of revelation is identical with the Omega of evolution, then by whatever means the culmination of God's plan of salvation for the human race is accomplished, it must in some way already be present in the life, death, and resurrection of Jesus of Nazareth. Mooney (1964), an eminent and insightful scholar of Teilhard's writings, comes to the following conclusion:

> In the Person of Jesus the real Omega took flesh and became part of that evolutionary current for which he himself is responsible...all the great Christological events must somehow be obedient to evolution's most fundamental law. Somehow we must be able to speak of a genesis which is Christic as well as a genesis which is cosmic, and in some sense we must be able to speak of them both as ultimately one and the same. It is precisely to speak in such a way, while yet remaining faithful to the

testimony of revelation, which is the aim of Teilhard de Chardin's Christology. (Mooney, 1964:63)

Communion with God through Earth

A most significant theme that kept recurring in Teilhard's writings throughout his life and which reappeared in his final essay written on April 9, 1955, the day before he died, was an urgent plea (U. King, 1996:2). His deeply felt desire expressed once again an urgent pastoral need for "'evangelization of a new age." He recognized the importance of finding a "'new understanding of the meaning of holiness, a new way of embodying the ideal of Christian perfection" in his world of twentieth-century science, technology, and globalization.

Teilhard expressed a mystical perspective on a solution in this word of advice: "Christians must learn to perceive and revere the sacredness of matter and the cosmos; the experience of the cosmos is a necessary dimension of human experience that must be integrated into the Christian faith." What Teilhard had in mind is a form of creation mysticism that he called "*a communion with God through earth*," "*a new synthesis between the forward and the upward*." The "new mysticism" that Teilhard spoke of is "a communion with God through earth" (U. King, 1997:87) in which the human being is united with the Absolute, with God, by means of the unification of the universe (Teilhard 1970:56), a concept linked to creation theology. Teilhard considered this new mysticism as a dynamic transformational process in which the person participates actively. He speaks of it as a "mysticism of evolution" and a "mysticism of action."

Ursula King points out that the time of postmodernity for which Teilhard was writing was one full of opportunity:

In an earlier age when Christian religious ideals still informed the entire culture, the human being was primarily understood in relation to the Divine, to God. The dominant scientific approach of today tends to relate the human being primarily to the animal and life worlds of our natural environment and that [in turn] to God—[these] need to be combined and linked with each other in a way that is new and culturally transformative and creative....Perhaps it is the very questions and problems raised by modernity, and the possibilities opening up with the new postmodern perspectives that will provide us with the opportunities for developing a truly holistic and transformative spirituality. (U. King, 1997:4)

Creation of Earth and Universe

Divine creation was established as a basic theological doctrine by the Council of Nicaea in 325 AD and was given primacy in the beginning of the Catholic Church's profession of faith as a fundamental tenet in Christian theology.

In the Nicene Creed Christians from the early days of the Church have affirmed that "we believe in one God, the Father, the Almighty, maker of heaven and earth, of all that is seen and unseen." Therefore believers from the earliest part of the Christian Era and Jews as well, as we know from the Hebrew Scriptures, have held that God is ultimately responsible for the existence of the entire material universe. Today, as was never possible before space travel and satellite photography, the Earth and Universe are objects of wonder and beauty as well as the object of scientific study. The Eastern Churches have preserved a long tradition of creation-theology....

More than a few Western Churches also have come to recognize that the sacramentality of all of creation is harmonious with Teilhard's mystical concept of "communion with God through earth." Expressed in a slightly different way Teilhard's phrase, *"the above with the ahead"*

(Cowell 2001:3, 5–6) expresses the fundamental core of his action-mysticism. By this he meant that it is impossible to rise to the *"above"* without moving *"ahead"*—or *"to progress ahead without rising toward the above"* (Cowell 2001; Cuénot, 1965:369), in reality an *"on-going creation theology."* The phrase *"above"* and *"from above"* so meaningful to Teilhard's *"new mysticism"* is actually a time-honored phrase that was familiar to Teilhard from Ignatius Loyola's Fourth Week of the *Spiritual Exercises.* (Skehan, 1991:155–56; 1994:77)

Teilhard's "new mysticism" is what we may refer to as a spirituality of ecotheology in the sense of looking on all of creation as sacred, an all-encompassing attitude of finding God in every aspect of nature and of human endeavor. "One who regards all of Creation as Sacred must necessarily think of the Earth with the kind of reverence that we would accord a lower case 'sacrament' because by sacrament is meant a 'sign' pointing to God's action in our lives" (Skehan, 2005:31).

Teilhard's attitude was that all Creation is sacred; that the entire lives of human beings are significant because we participate in creation-so-to-speak not only by "building the earth but the entire cosmos." Based on his understanding of key passages of St. Paul, Teilhard envisioned that each of us, with Christ, serves as "co-creator" and "co-redeemer" of the Earth and Universe during our time and place on planet Earth (Skehan, 2001:45–52). These understandings impart a new appreciation of the link between the created world and our own "action-oriented" spirituality of "building the Earth and the Cosmos." (Skehan, 2005:31)

Teilhard's Influence on Research

Teilhard was first and foremost a Jesuit scientist and priest with an enormous appetite for exploration of the previously undiscovered. As a result he was forever discovering new doorways to knowledge and spirituality. What follows is only a sampling of the rich menu of Teilhard's pioneering discoveries. We here ask the question: "What has been Teilhard's influence on the geosciences and spirituality as well as a few related problems and opportunities to which he addressed himself?"

The influence of Teilhard's thought on scientific research necessarily varies with the particular discipline under discussion. As a Jesuit priest-geologist, I value greatly Teilhard's substantial contributions to basic research in field geology in a vast terrain which was relatively unknown when he first set foot there in 1921. In addition, a major contribution and influence was mapping of Pleistocene stratigraphy widely over large parts of China (Schmitz-Moorman, 1971 in 11 vols.) in behalf of firmly establishing basic principles of stratigraphy in that vast land. Teilhard's work and that of his collaborator of thirty-five years, George Barbour, were of special significance for stratigraphical, geologic, and paleontological research in China and other parts of Southeastern Asia and parts of Africa and Europe.

The following are a few selected areas in which Teilhard carried out pioneering work. The extent to which his excellent research in basic geology in China actually influenced later research globally is unknown because China has been largely closed off to the outside world of geology and paleontology, to the best of my knowledge, since Teilhard left China in 1947. However, as China opens up to the international scientific community even now and in the future we may see something of a renaissance in those fields. When a higher degree of mutual trust comes about between nations, I believe that Teilhard's influence and that of the China Geological Survey is likely to be profound.

Stratigraphy

Teilhard's influence on field and theoretical contributions in the branch of geology that deals with the study of the distribution and relations of both continental and local scales of stratified rocks in portions of China occurred at a critical time in the evolution of the methodology.

Influence on Precision Age Dating of Strata in behalf of Age Dating of Life Forms

Teilhard recognized, as did many others, that a focus on careful stratigraphic correlations and more precise age-dating methods are of critical importance for determination of ages of life forms and especially of human fossils contained in the various layers, especially those of the Pleistocene epoch (about 600,000 years ago). Teilhard was always mindful of the importance of developing more precise dating methods to mark especially the appearance of the earliest human as well as building a time-space framework for locating forms of life of whatever age.

Teilhard regarded himself "first of all as a geologist, secondarily as a paleontologist, specializing in mammals, and only thirdly as a prehistorian and anthropologist" (Cuénot, 1965:91). When Teilhard went to China and was invited to serve as advisor to the director of the China Geological Survey and to help plan geological research over all of China, he identified clearly the need for continent-wide stratigraphic correlations in order to achieve more precise age dates for life forms including humans. As a result Teilhard's horizons were greatly expanded in terms of the vast areas involved in the great Asiatic continent, and the pressing need and opportunity that then existed to carry out careful stratigraphic correlations and age determination studies with the upper Cenozoic strata (from about 65 million years ago to the present).

Teilhard's Mysticism of Scientific Research

In a reversal from traditional mysticism of unknowing, Teilhard began to focus on a mysticism of knowing "particularly as knowing relates to scientific discovery....Religion and Science are the two conjugated faces or phases of one and the same complete act of knowledge" (King, 1981:vii). In commenting on its meaning, Thomas King explains its deeper significance. He states that Teilhard's profound understanding of the meaning of the complete act of knowledge is revealed in "his exuberant claim that in the very act of scientifically achieving, he knew God." He follows this by stating that Teilhard began writing a theology of process "when human knowledge is in process, God is found in the act of knowing."

As a Jesuit geologist, nurtured over the past sixty-five years by the *Spiritual Exercises* of St. Ignatius, founder of the Society of Jesus, I sought to find the common ground that would be calculated to enrich both aspects of my life, namely, my research and teaching in geology and a spirituality or mysticism that would enrich both.

Harvey Egan, SJ, and Thomas King, SJ, both scholars of mysticism, have written at length about Teilhard's mysticism and especially about the fact that there is a mysticism of scientific research (Skehan, 2005). About 1973 in reading Harvey Egan's book, *What Are They Saying About Mysticism*, I found a statement in the chapter on "A Future Mysticism" that linked science and mysticism. Egan quoted the Jesuit theologian, Bernard Lonergan, as saying: "Science and Religion have much in common, namely fidelity to the transcendental precepts." I came to understand that this utterly simple statement has profound implications, namely, that whoever responds faithfully to the "basic dynamism of the mind to be attentive, to be reasonable, to be responsible, and to be in love" is an authentic person.

In speaking of activities involving a geologist practicing his science, I interpret that last phrase, "to be in love," to mean that one who is wholeheartedly dedicated to seeking geological truth is thereby acting as an authentic scholar. Basically this means "theology and the 'secular sciences' have in common the requirements of fidelity to the transcendental precepts." Without at the moment going into more detail regarding the transcendental precepts, I find that the scientist who is faithful to the transcendental precepts is engaged in an activity and achieves results that are the product not only of intelligence but of personal integrity in carrying out the research (Skehan, 2005:192–97).

Teilhard was concerned with what I refer to as a spirituality of scientific research. He developed many of the ideas integral to a theology of scientific research. Teilhardian scholars have combed through all of the writings of Teilhard and pulled together at least the framework of his mysticism of scientific research. Many of Teilhard's key ideas, such as the "Cosmic Sense, the sense of the universal, the Sense of the Earth or the Sense of Plenitude" he regarded as the common basis of mysticism (King, 1981:4).

Teilhard's Perspective on Studies
of Love and Sexual Attraction

Teilhard wrote:

Love is the most universal, the most tremendous, and the most mysterious of cosmic forces. After centuries of tentative effort, social institutions have externally diked it and canalized it. Moralists have tried to submit it to rules. Socially, in science, business, and public affairs, men pretend not to know it, though under the surface it is everywhere. Huge, ubiquitous, and always unsubdued—this wild force seems to have defeated all hopes of understanding and governing it. We are conscious of it, but all we ask of it is to amuse us, or not harm us. Is it possible for humanity to continue to live and grow without asking itself how much truth and energy it is losing by neglecting the incredible power of love? In its most primitive forms, love is hard to distinguish from molecular forces. Little by little it becomes distinct, though still confused for a very long time with reproduction. No longer only a unique and periodic attraction for purposes of material fertility, but an unbounded and continuous possibility of contact between minds rather than bodies. Preoccupation with preserving the species gradually dissolves in the greater intoxication of two people creating a world. (Teilhard, 1969:32–34)

I do not know whether Teilhard has in fact had a substantial influence on research into the societal and religious implications of love and sexual attraction. However, his brief discussion of the implications of it has established an important although brief groundwork for significant research and discussion of one of society's most far-reaching problems. There are numerous other topics of deep concern to individuals and to society in general that are not only of great concern but are enigmatic as far as solutions to often pressing problems are concerned. One of these is love and sexual attraction, which deals both with the noblest of human emotions and also the most destructive when misdirected.

Teilhard's Perspective on Suffering and Transforming It into Spiritual Energy

This is a two-part discussion (Teilhard de Chardin, 1970). Suffering and the cause of suffering had been given much attention in public discussions without, as far as I am aware, providing totally beneficial, satisfactory, or inspiring light on the subject. However, Teilhard has emphasized the religious component of Jesus and the cross that is in my view a uniquely appropriate solution. The fact that Teilhard had suffered so many setbacks throughout his career makes it possible to point to his manner of accepting what must have been acute, personal, psychological suffering in many aspects of his life.

Teilhard sketched a prevailing attitude toward suffering:

Consider the total suffering of the whole earth at every moment. If we were able to...gauge its volume, to weigh, count, analyze it—what an astronomic mass, what a terrifying total! And, from physical torture to moral agonies, how subtle a range of shades of misery!...And, if only all the pain were mixed with all the joy of the world, who can say on which side balance would settle, on that of pain or that of joy?

Yes, the more the human being becomes human, the more deeply ingrained and the more serious—in his flesh, in his nerves, in his mind—becomes the problem of evil. Evil that has to be understood and evil that has to be borne.

A sounder view of the universe...is now providing us with the beginning of an answer to this problem. We are realizing that within the vast process of arrangement from which life emerges, every success is necessarily paid for by a large percentage of failures. One cannot progress in being without paying a mysterious tribute of tears, blood, and sin. It is hardly surprising then...when we see it from this angle, suffering in all its forms and all its degrees is (at least to some extent) no more than a natural consequence of the movement by which we were brought into being.

...[I]s it not psychologically that we discover, in addition, some positive value in this painful wastage ...that will transfigure it and make it permanently acceptable? Of that there can be no doubt...it is here that comes into play...the astounding Christian revolution of a suffering which...can be transformed into an expression of love and a principle of union: suffering that is first

treated as an enemy...to be defeated; then suffering vig-
orously fought against to the bitter end; and yet...suffer-
ing rationally accepted and cordially welcomed inasmuch
as by forcing us out of our egocentrism...it can supercenter us upon God. Yes, indeed: suffering in obscurity,
suffering with all its repulsiveness, elevated for the humblest of patients into a supremely active principle of universal humanization and divinization—such is seen to be
at its peak the supreme spiritual dynamic force, born of
the cross. (Teilhard, 1970:247–48)

The Core of Teilhard's Spirituality

Teilhard's spirituality, which I think is correctly described as
a mysticism of action, must have shaped the activities of his
everyday life and especially the quality of his research and writing as well as his professional and personal life. He must have
been motivated to an extraordinary degree not only to have
accomplished his prodigious geological research in the harsh cli-
mate and terrain conditions of China, as well as to have written
a large number of sublime essays and other compositions.

The following essay, written in 1943 just four years before his
debilitating heart attack in 1947, sums up succinctly a number of
the concepts or themes at the core of Teilhard's "evolutionary"
spirituality. In it Teilhard refers to a passage from a related 1943
essay in which he is preoccupied with our "psychological need...to
love human progress before"...we "can dedicate ourselves to it
completely." It is clear from these two essays that an aspect of the
love that he was describing was a heartfelt "enthusiasm." He
underscores the point that "the source of a universal love...can
only come from Christianity, which alone can teach us how to love
deeply...a universe whose very evolution has been impregnated
with love." A translation by Christopher Mooney of Teilhard's

essay on his concept of a mysticism of action, both short-term and long-term, is as follows:

> Because everything in the universe is in fact ultimately moving towards Christ-Omega; because cosmogenesis, moving in its totality through anthropogenesis, ultimately shows itself to be a Christogenesis; because of this, I say, it follows that the real is charged with a divine presence in the entirety of its tangible layers. As the mystics knew and felt, everything becomes physically and literally lovable in God; and conversely, God can be possessed and loved in everything around us....I repeat, if the whole movement of the world is in the service of a Christogenesis (which is another way of saying that Christ is attainable in his fullness only at the end and summit of cosmic evolution), *then clearly we can draw near to him and possess him only in and through the effort to bring all to fulfillment and synthesis in him* (emphasis mine: JWS). And this is the reason that life's general ascent towards higher consciousness as well as the whole of human endeavor enter organically and by right into the preoccupations and aspirations of charity (divine love).

Teilhard goes on to further explain the core of his action-mysticism, which underlies his entire thought about the relationship of the incarnation and, implicitly, the mystery of the Holy Eucharist to all of the spheres of cosmic evolution:

> We have seen that Christ, by reason of his position as Omega of the world, represents a focus towards whom and in whom everything converges. In other words, he appears as One in whom all reality...establishes union and contact in the only direction possible: the line of centers. What can this mean except that *every action, as*

soon as it is oriented towards him, takes on, without any change in itself, the psychic character of a centre-to-centre relationship, that is to say, of an act of love....At first the Christian aspired only to be able to love...*while* acting. Now he [or she] is aware of being able to love *in* acting, that is to say...can unite...directly to the divine Centre through action itself, no matter what form such action takes. In him all activity is, if I may use the expression, 'amorized'....There are those today... among whom the lived conjunction of the two ideas of Incarnation and evolution has led to the creation of a synthesis of the personal and the universal. For the first time in history [human beings] are capable not only of understanding and serving, but of *loving evolution*. (Mooney, 1964:161–62)

Bibliography

Appleton-Weber, Sarah, ed. and trans. *The Human Phenomenon* Brighton, England: Sussex Academic Press, 1999.

Barbour, G. B. *In the Field with Teilhard de Chardin*. New York: Herder and Herder, 1965.

Cowell, Sion. *The Teilhard Lexicon: Understanding the Language, Terminology and Vision of the writings of Pierre Teilhard de Chardin*. Brighton, UK/Portland, OR: Sussex Academic Press, 2001.

Cuénot, C. *Teilhard de Chardin: A Biographical Study*. Baltimore: Helicon Press, Inc., 1965.

De Lubac, Henri. *The Religion of Teilhard de Chardin*. New York: William Collins Sons, Inc., 1967. Originally published in French under the title *La pensée religieuse du Père Teilhard de Chardin*, Editions Montaigne, 1962.

De Lubac, Henri. *Teilhard de Chardin: The Man and His Meaning*. New York: Hawthorn Books, 1965.

Egan, Harvey D. *An Anthology of Christian Mysticism*. Collegeville, MN: The Liturgical Press, 1991.

Egan, Harvey D. *Ignatius Loyola the Mystic*. The Way of the Christian Mystics. Wilmington, DE: Michael Glazier, 1987.

Egan, Harvey D. *The Future of a Tradition*. New York: Pueblo, 1984.

Egan, Harvey D. *What Are They Saying About Mysticism?* New York: Paulist Press, 1982.

Fleming, D. L. *The Spiritual Exercises of St. Ignatius: A Literal Translation and a Contemporary Reading*. St. Louis: The Institute of Jesuit Sources, 1978.

King, T. M. *Teilhard's Mysticism of Knowing*. New York: The Seabury Press, 1982.

King, T. M. *Teilhard's Mass: Approaches to "The Mass on the World."* New York: Paulist Press, 2005.

King, Ursula. *Spirit of Fire: The Life and Vision of Teilhard de Chardin*. Maryknoll, NY: Orbis Books, 1996.

King, Ursula. *The Spirit of One Earth: Reflections on Teilhard de Chardin and Global Spirituality*. New York: Paragon House, 1989.

King, Ursula. *Christ in All Things: Exploring Spirituality with Teilhard de Chardin*. Maryknoll, NY: Orbis Books, 1997.

Lonergan, Bernard J. F. *Method in Theology*. New York: Herder and Herder, 1972.

Lukas, Mary, and Ellen Lukas. *Teilhard*. New York: McGraw Hill, 1981; originally published by Doubleday, 1977.

MacDonnell, Joseph F. *Jesuit Geometers*. St. Louis: The Institute of Jesuit Sources, St. Louis University, 1989.

MacDonnell, Joseph F. *Jesuit Family Album: Sketches of Chivalry from the Early Society*. Fairfield, CT: Fairfield University, 1997.

McMenamin, Mark A. S. *Evolution of the Noosphere*. Teilhard Studies, 42. New York: American Teilhard Association for the Future of Man, 2001.

McMenamin, Mark A. S. "The Ptychopariod Trilobite Skehanos gen. nov. from the Middle Cambrian of Avalonian Massachusetts and the Carolina Slate belt, USA." *Northeastern Geology and Environmental Sciences*, 2002, 24, (4), 276–81.

McMenamin, Mark A. S., and D. L. S. McMenamin. *The Emergence of Animals: The Cambrian Breakthrough*. New York: Columbia University Press, 1990.

Mooney, Christopher F. *Teilhard de Chardin and the Mystery of Christ*. New York: Harper and Row, 1964.

Pope John Paul II. *Ecclesia de Eucharistia*. Encyclical, *Origins*, v. 32. no. 46, #8, 2003: 755–67.

Pope John Paul II. *Gift and Mystery: On the Fiftieth Anniversary of My Priesthood*. New York: Doubleday, 1996.

Ratzinger, Joseph Cardinal. *The Spirit of the Liturgy*. San Francisco: Ignatius Press, 2000.

Schmitz-Moorman, Nicole and Karl, eds. *Pierre Teilhard de Chardin, L'Oeuvre Scientifique*. Olten and Freiburg im Breisgau, Walter Verlag, 1971.

Skehan, James W. "The Role and Importance of Research and Publication in Church-Related Schools." In *Science/Technology Education in Church-Related Colleges and Universities*, edited by Robert A. Brungs, 110–25. St. Louis: ITEST Faith/Science Press, 1990.

Skehan, James W. *Place Me with Your Son: Ignatian Spirituality in Everyday Life*. Third edition. Washington, D.C.: Georgetown University Press, 1991.

Skehan, James W. *Place Me with Your Son: Ignatian Spirituality in Everyday Life*. Director's Guide to third edition. Washington, D.C.: Georgetown University Press, 1994.

Skehan, James W. "Assembly and Dispersal of Supercontinents: The View from Avalon." *Journal of Geodynamics*, 23 (3/4), 1997: 237–62.

Skehan, James W. "Spiritual Foundations for Ethics in the Geosciences." Unpublished Keynote Address to the Geological Society of America's (GSA) Presidential Penrose Conference, "Ethics in the Geosciences," The Welches, Oregon, 1997. 16 pp.

Skehan, James W. *Praying with Teilhard de Chardin*. Winona, MN: St. Mary's Press, 2001.

Skehan, J. W. "Exploring Teilhard's 'New Mysticism': 'Building the Cosmos.' *Journal of Ecotheology, Religion, Nature and the Environment*, v.10.1, no. 1, 11–34, 2005.

Teilhard de Chardin, Pierre. "Cosmic Life (An Essay)," 1916. Published in *Writings in Time of War*, 13–71, New York: Harper and Row, 1965.

Teilhard de Chardin, Pierre. *The Mass on the World*. New York: Harper and Row, Publishers, 1923.

Teilhard de Chardin, Pierre. *The Phenomenon of Man*. New York: Harper Torchbooks, Harper & Row, Publishers, 1959.

Teilhard de Chardin, Pierre. *The Divine Milieu*. New York: Harper Colophon Books, Harper & Row, Publishers, 1960.

Teilhard de Chardin, Pierre. *Letters from a Traveller*. New York: Harper and Row, Publishers, 1962.

Teilhard de Chardin, Pierre. *The Future of Man*. New York: Harper and Row, Publishers, 1964.

Teilhard de Chardin, Pierre. *Writings in Time of War*. New York: Harper and Row, Publishers, 1965.

Teilhard de Chardin, Pierre. *How I Believe*. New York: Harper and Row, 1969.

Teilhard de Chardin, Pierre. "The Spiritual Energy of Suffering." In *Activation of Energy*. New York: Harcourt Brace Jovanovich, 1970.

Vernadsky, V. I. *The Biosphere*. 1926. English translation by David Langmuir. Annotations by Mark McMenamin. New York: Copernicus, 1998.

CHAPTER NINE

Teilhard's Two Energies[1]

Harold J. Morowitz,[2] Nicole Schmitz-Moormann, and James Salmon, SJ

No concept of Teilhard de Chardin has been subject to greater criticism and derision than "The Problem of the Two Energies." A major scientific question for Teilhard was the organization of energy during cosmic and biological evolution. The purpose of this essay is to point to the validity of Teilhard's intuition as demonstrated by subsequent developments in statistical mechanics and information theory. The derision noted above was at times mean-spirited and did not show an understanding of the deep thermodynamic and statistical mechanics that underlie the difficult problems of bioenergetics that troubled Teilhard.

To understand the roots of the paradox faced by Teilhard, we go back in the mid-1800s, when in the same decade (1850–1860) Darwin and Wallace developed the theory of evolution, and Clausius and Kelvin independently stated the second law of thermodynamics. These two principles immediately appeared to be in contradiction; physics seemed to be saying the world was becoming more and more disorganized while biology seemed to be saying that the world of life was becoming more and more organized and complexified.

Although this conundrum was solved by Ludwig Boltzmann in 1886, his solution was ignored by physicists and probably unknown to most biologists. Teilhard was probably unaware of Boltzmann's words:

The general struggle of living beings for existence is therefore not a struggle for materials nor energy (that is present in every body and in large quantity as heat, unfortunately not interchangeable) but a struggle for entropy [some authors refer to this phenomenon as negentropy] that becomes available in the transition of the energy from the hot sun to the cold earth. To exploit this transition as much as possible the plants spread out the immeasurable areas of their leaves and force the solar energy in an as yet unexplored way to carry out chemical syntheses of which we have no idea in our laboratories. (Broda 1978, 3)

Most biologists were either unaware or did not face the resolution of the entropy-evolution problem until the second half of the twentieth century, and some are still unaware of it. Teilhard over his career faced this issue.

Part I of this essay indicates Teilhard's groping with this problem, and his solutions without final resolution. Then in Part II we trace the historical development of a noetic aspect of energy within the sciences of thermodynamics, statistical mechanics, and information theory. Finally, we conclude by pointing out the remarkable prescience of Teilhard's intuition, despite its scientific ambiguity.

Part I

The concept of energy in evolution was a constant theme in private journals and essays of Teilhard. His scientific research, including ten volumes of technical publications in geology and paleontology, supported his intuition that matter-energy is more than purely inert stuff. Observations and extensive readings about communication in nature, especially among organisms, led to the realization that, besides the obvious emergence of consciousness and freedom, there is an increasing flow of information taking place during evolution. It is significant to recall that most essays and the private journals referred to here were never published until after Teilhard's death in 1955.

In the introduction to her splendid new editing and correct translation of *The Human Phenomenon*, Sarah Appleton Weber writes: "The subject of the human phenomenon was developed by Teilhard in three earlier essays of 1925, 1926, and 1930, and it became the pivotal point for all his thought (*Oeuvres*, XIII, ff.)"[3] (Teilhard 1999, xviii). By 1938–1940 Teilhard was forced to clarify his thoughts about energy when he finalized previous drafts of his worldview. He noted how nothing is more obscure scientifically than spiritual energy. On the other hand, he assumes the objective work of the psyche is certain as the basis of ethics, and yet this interior power is so slight that the laws of mechanics could be understood without it.

Because of the inadequacy of the two laws of classical thermodynamics, of conservation and dissipation, to explain the human experience of energy, he proposes two aspects. "There is no doubt that material energy and spiritual energy hold together and are prolonged by *something*. Ultimately, *somehow or other*, there must be only a single energy at play in the world" (Teilhard 1999, 29).

> "To think we must eat," once again. But on the other hand, so many different thoughts come out of the same piece of bread!...The two energies—physical and psychical—spread respectively through the external and internal layers of the world behave on the whole in the same way. They are constantly associated and somehow flow into each other. But it seems impossible to establish a simple correspondence between their curves. (Teilhard 1999, 30)

This association of a noetic aspect to a purely material (traditional) understanding of energy forced Teilhard to introduce a new model:

We shall assume that all energy is essentially psychic. But we shall add that in each individual element this fundamental energy is divided into two distinct components: a *tangential energy* making the element interdependent with all elements of the same order in the universe as itself (that is of the same complexity and same "centricity"): and a *radial energy* attracting the element in the direction of an ever more complex and centered state, toward what is ahead.*

*Note, by the way, that the less centered an element is (that is, the weaker its radial energy), the more its tangential energy is shown through powerful mechanical effects. Between strongly centered particles (that is, particles with a high radial energy), the tangential seems to become "interiorized" and to disappear, in the eyes of physics. [The * refers to a footnote added by Teilhard.] (Teilhard 1999, 30)

Teilhard cautions the reader about this model to understand energy. He writes that the purpose is to offer an example of the line of research that might be adopted for a science of nature and the kind of explanation that could be pursued.

"More naturalist than physicist" (Teilhard 1999, 11) it seems Teilhard's model introduces a potential research program that bridges science and philosophy to investigate "the axis and arrow of evolution" (Teilhard 1999, 7). He calls this new "science of nature" hyperphysics:

Take any major book written about the world by one of the great modern scientists such as Poincaré, Einstein, Jeans, and the others. It is impossible to attempt a general scientific interpretation of the universe without *seeming* to intend to explain it right to the end. But only take a closer look at it, and you will see this "hyperphysics" still is not metaphysics. (Teilhard 1999, 2)

His studies in philosophy and theology early in his career supported an intuition of two energies as it developed in Teilhard's own mind. Along with early versions of *The Human Phenomenon*, comparison of the traditional energy of physics to a psychical energy, especially human energy, is found in other early essays. For example:

- in "The Spirit of the Earth" in 1931: "Love is the most universal; the most tremendous and the most mysterious of the cosmic forces" (Teilhard 1969, 32), and "Love is a sacred reserve of energy; it is like the blood of spiritual evolution" (Teilhard 1969, 34).

- in "Christianity in the World" in 1933: "Through man, an ocean of free energy (an energy as real and as 'cosmic' as the others with which physics is concerned) sets out to cover the earth" (Teilhard 1968, 99).

- in "The Evolution of Chastity" in 1934: "The day will come when, after harnessing the ether, the winds, the tides, gravitation, we shall harness for God the energies of love. And on that day, for the second time in the history of the world, man will have discovered fire" (Teilhard 1975, 86–87).

- in "Human Energy" in 1937: "By the energy of man I here mean the always increasing portion of cosmic energy at present undergoing the recognizable influence of the centres of human energy" (Teilhard 1969, 115).

Teilhard finished an essay in December 1944, "Centrology," that manifests advancement in his thought about two energies. The essay expands and clarifies the development of his intuition between 1938 and 1944. The essay is fundamental to Teilhard's understanding of both energy and matter.[4]

"Centrology" clarifies the interdependence of each "individual element" of the same complexity (and therefore centricity) in *The Human Phenomenon*.

1. As the foundation for the whole edifice of propositions that follow we have an intuition and two observations:

a. *The intuition*: In the swarming multiplicity of living elements (monocellular and polycellular) which make up the biosphere, we find an authentic continuation of the granular (atomic, molecular) structure of the universe. In consequence, if the human body is restored to its position in the cosmic corpuscular series, it is simply a "super-molecule": once we see it in this light, we are in the happy position of being able to distinguish in that super-molecule, the properties in a "magnified" state, of *every* molecule.

b. *The observations*: Man, the final product of planetary evolution, is both supremely *complex* in his physico-chemical organization (measured by the brain), and at the same time, viewed in his psychism, supremely *free* and *conscious*. (Teilhard 1970, 101)

Because of an innate fondness for diagrammatic portraits of his thought, Teilhard clarifies the "intuition" in Fig. 1:

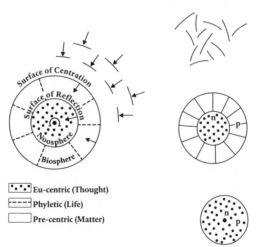

Fig. 1: Complexification Process

He calls it a "Diagram symbolizing the principal phases of centrogenesis (convergence of the universe along its axis of centro-complexity or personalization)," from Pre-centric (Matter) to Eu-centric (Thought) (Teilhard 1970, 100). The three principal zones of the evolutionary process are represented that engender consciousness and reflection. The left sketch outlines the general process, and the right sketch explains each stage of the process in more detail. The two diagrams subdivide the zones of concentric isospheres that represent three levels in the process of evolution: preliving (Matter), Biosphere (from Greek, βίος meaning "life"), and the "magnified" state of reflection (Thought), what Teilhard calls Noosphere (from Greek νους, meaning "mind"). This division of zones expands and clarifies his general understanding of the meaning of "elements" in his introduction of two energies in *The Human Phenomenon*. The top sketch on the right in Figure 1 illustrates fragments of preliving matter. Note that the fragments are open at each end, offering a sort of curvature. At this level of disjunction of fragments, there is only a disposition to come together and to fit in with one another—not by intention—but through the play of chance. This aspect of matter again recalls his division of the two energies in *The Human Phenomenon* in all elements of matter:

> At every degree of size and complexity, cosmic particles or grains are not simply, as physics has recognized, centres of universal dynamic radiation: all of them, in addition (rather like man), have and represent a small "within" (however diffuse or even fragmentary it may be…in which is reflected, at a more or less rudimentary stage, a particular representation of the world: in relation to themselves they are psychic centres of the universe. In other words, consciousness is a universal molecular property; and the molecular state of the world is a manifestation of the pluralized state of some potentiality of universal consciousness. (Teilhard 1999, 101)

Just as Teilhard noted in his footnote to the introduction of the two energies in *The Human Phenomenon*, quoted above, tangential energy has the dominant role in these preliving fragments, although the psychic energy aspect is always present, no matter how small the element. Although his accuracy of measurements is according to 1944 standards, the principle remains:

> While it [consciousness] is completely imperceptible to our observational methods below an atomic complexity of 10^5 (the virus), it can be plainly detected when we reach that of the cell (10^{10}); but it enters its major developments only in the brains of large mammals (10^{20}), in other words when we have atomic groupings astronomic in order. (Teilhard 1970, 102)

The "intuition" that is developed in "Centrology" links the description of physical and psychic energies with the description of tangential and radial energies respectively in *The Human Phenomenon*. Teilhard continues to maintain:

> The behaviour of these two energies (physical and psychic) is so completely different, and their phenomenal manifestations are so completely irreducible, that we might believe they derive from two entirely independent ways of explaining the world. (Teilhard 1970, 120)

However, he continues to see a hidden connection between the two energies:

> Nevertheless, since they both carry through their evolution in the same universe, in the same temporal dimension, there must surely be some hidden relationship which links them together in their development. (Teilhard 1970, 120)

The application of isospheres to evolution in "Centrology" proposes a solution to a problem he found in his more simple description of tangential and radial energies in *The Human Phenomenon*, where he wrote:

> The only difficulty with this perspective, where tangential energy represents the abbreviated view of "energy" habitually considered by science, is to explain the play of tangential arrangements so that it is in harmony with the laws of thermodynamics. (Teilhard 1999, 31)

At this point in *The Human Phenomenon* he was seeking to recognize:

> The fundamental discovery, that all bodies derive, *by arrangement*, from one initial corpuscular type is the flash that lights up the history of the universe for our eyes. From the beginning, matter has, in its own way, obeyed the great biological law of "complexification" (a law we shall return to again and again). (Teilhard 1999, 17–18)

In "Centrology" Teilhard questions his intuition, although he is convinced of a need for more detail than was offered by physics to understand the two energies experienced in an evolutionary world:

> From the point of view of centrogenesis, in short, everything floats on a tide of convergent psychic energy which rises both qualitatively and quantitatively from isosphere to isosphere, in step with personalization. This being so, what is the relationship between this interior energy, always increasing and always more "amorized," and the goddess of energy worshipped by physicists—an energy that is always constant and at the same time (by dissipation) always more "calorized"?[5] (Teilhard 1970, 120)

To answer his question, he returns to the distinction between pre-living cosmic elements (Matter) and elements inside the surfaces of centration in Figure 1 (Life and Thought):

Omega cannot act *internally* (nor, in consequence, by attraction *ahead*) on elements of the first type, since their centres are not yet individualized. It must, therefore, set them in motion *a retro* and by some sort of external impulse. Everything, *in fact*, behaves as if this setting in motion bore the characteristic of a single impulse, productive of a definite "quantum" of actions; this is precisely the energy, subject to conservation and dissipation with which physics is concerned. (Teilhard 1970, 121)

In general, Teilhard has seen Omega as a point of attraction in the universe and so he sees a contradiction of inserting the motion *a retro*.[6] He adds in a footnote:

This is one explanation, but is there not another, which is simpler and fits in more smoothly? Let us admit that the attraction of Omega can make itself felt internally, even in the fragmentary (pre-living) centres (psychic energy, cf. above). In that case could not physical energy (and its over-all conservation) be interpreted as the statistical "by-product" of a great number of elementary psychic energies (energies of atoms) which combine tangentially...with practically no variation in number— just as the regularity of physical laws (the determinisms of matter) is explained by the statistical play of a great number of infinitesimal, inorganic, free impulses...? From this point of view, one would have to say that everything in the universe (back to the most distant isospheres) moves in one and the same internal stream, emanating from Omega: *physical energy* being no more than *materialized psychic energy*. (Teilhard 1970, 121)

To summarize, all energy is psychic energy in *The Human Phenomenon* and is composed of two parts, radial (the axial energy of evolution) and tangential (the energy of physics). The two parts of energy seem to be equal at this stage. Four years later in *Centrology*, Teilhard classifies the two energies into psychic and physical components. However, the physical component is now "materialized psychic energy." Thus all energy is essentially psychic, although energy continues to be made up of two components. On May 3, 1945, Teilhard wrote in his journal "Doubler la Centrologie d'une Rythmologie? ("Rythmanalyse") (*Unpublished Journals of Teilhard de Chardin*). This intention to apply the synthetic vision of two energies in "Centrology" to the process of interiorization and unification of matter is manifested in succeeding relevant essays: "The Analysis of Life," dated 10 June 1945, Peking (Teilhard 1970, 131–39); "Life and the Planets," a lecture at the French Embassy in Peking 10 March 1945, and published in the Jesuit journal *Etudes*, May 1946 (Teilhard 1964, 97–123); and "The Planetisation of Mankind," dated 25 December 1945, Peking, and published in *Cahiers du Monde Nouveau*, August–September 1946 (Teilhard 1964, 124–39).

Teilhard never stopped thinking about the issue of two energies to explain evolution. His private journals and later essays reveal that he also never was fully satisfied with his definition of the two energies.

In a 1954 essay, "The Singularities of the Human Species," Teilhard reveals again his concern about the two aspects of energy (Teilhard 1965, 208–73). He distinguishes psychical or radial energy from physical or tangential energy, the former "escaping from entropy," the latter obeying the laws of thermodynamics. Here two energies are not directly transformable but are interdependent of one another in their function and evolution. His concept of the radial aspect of energy is to increase with the arrangement of the tangential, but the tangential only arranging itself when prompted by the radial. Thus the fundamental interpretation of the two energies that includes a noetic aspect is retained and does not seem to be very different from the original analysis in *The Human Phenomenon* (cf. Teilhard 1999, 30).

The depth of Teilhard's knowledge of classical thermodynamics is uncertain. Although he discussed and used the formalities of chance and statistics within evolutionary theory, there is no indication of his familiarity with formalities used in statistical mechanics. He comments in the private journals about his readings of many contemporary scientific authors. His positive review of Erwin Schrödinger's *What Is Life?* was published in "Revue des Livres" in 1950 (275–76). Reading Norbert Wiener's *Cybernetics* in 1951 stimulated and verified his interest in information as a component of the evolutionary process. In a 1953 essay, "The Activation of Human Energy," he refers to a review by Louis de Broglie, "La Cybernétiqué," in *Nouvelle Revue Française* (1 July 1953, 84), and concludes:

> We still persist in regarding the physical as constituting the "true" phenomenon in the universe, and the psychic as a sort of epiphenomenon. However, as suspected (if I understand them correctly) by such coolly objective minds as Louis de Broglie and Léon Brillouin, surely, if we really wish to unify the real, we should completely reverse the values—that is, we should consider the whole of thermodynamics.... An interior energy of unification (true energy) gradually emerging, under the influence of organization, from the superficial system of action and reactions that make up the physico-chemical.

In other words, there is no longer just one type of energy in the world: There are two different energies—one axial, increasing, and irreversible, and the other peripheral or tangential, constant, and reversible: and these two energies are linked together in "arrangement," but without nevertheless being able either to form a compound or directly to be transformed into one another, because they operate at different levels.

We may well wonder whether, if we refuse to accept such a duality (which is no dualism!) in the stuff of things, it is scientifically conceivable that a universe can function, from the moment when it *reflects itself upon itself*. (Teilhard 1970, 393)

The suggestion to reconsider a "gradual emerging" energy, axial in nature, within "the whole of thermodynamics" indicates the value of Teilhard's long-held intuition. His propositions about two energies that were based on his scientific research and experience, observing communication in nature, had reached a level of maturity that also seems to validate what has been subsequently shown below.

Part II

In this part we develop the thermodynamics, statistical mechanics, and information theory from 1875 to 1957 that provides a background to understand Teilhard's two-energies viewpoint.

In a series of papers *published* from October 1875 to May 1876, Josiah Willard Gibbs developed the foundations of chemical thermodynamics (Gibbs 1875–76, 108–248). He introduced a number of energy functions including (in Gibbs notation):

$$\chi = u + pv$$
$$\zeta = u - TS + pv$$

T, S, u, p, and v are the conventional thermodynamic variables: temperature, entropy, total energy, pressure, and volume. The conservation of energy is usually given as the first law of thermodynamics, $du = dq - pdv$ (change of energy is heat in, dq, minus work done, pdv). We can combine the above to get

$$d\chi = dq + vdp$$

χ is now called the enthalpy and at constant pressure measures the heat change. In modern usage χ is usually noted as H. ζ is now called the Gibbs Free Energy and is represented as G.

$$d\zeta = dq + vdp - TdS - SdT$$

At constant pressure and temperature this becomes

$d\zeta = dq - TdS$

or

$dG = dH - TdS$

G is the function used in biochemistry since its minimization for a system under consideration leads to global entropy maximization in accordance with the second law of thermodynamics. Note however as early as 1876 the Gibbs free energy could be represented as the sum of two terms: one, the calorimetric enthalpy, and the second dependent on the enigmatic negentropy, -S. As early as 1876, there were thus two components of energy within the formulation of conventional thermodynamics.

In the late 1800s Ludwig Boltzmann and Josiah Willard Gibbs created statistical mechanics that enabled the development of the equations of thermodynamics starting from molecular mechanics. In 1902 Gibbs (Gibbs 1902) introduced the thermodynamic probability of a state as

$W = N! / \Pi_e N_e!$

where e designates the eth element of phase space, and N_e the number of members of the ensemble in that state. An element of phase space was determined by the positions and momenta of all the atoms in the system. The ensemble consisted of the very large array of systems, macroscopically identical but varying in the microscopic details of the coordinates of the atoms. It is averaging over the ensemble that is the statistics of statistical mechanics. Gibbs then postulated that

$S = k \log W$

and was able to show that with the appropriate choice of k (now known as Boltzmann's constants) S is identical to the entropy of classical thermodynamics to within an additive constant. Then

$S = -k N \sum w_e \log w_e$

where $w_e = N_e / N$, and w_e is the probability of being associated with the eth element of phase space (Page 1929, 399).

With the development of quantum mechanics p_i is the probability of being in the ith quantum state and the entropy is

$$S = -k \sum p_i \log p_i$$

This provided an absolute value for the entropy and removed the additive constant.

In 1944 Erwin Schrödinger published *What Is Life?* in which he followed up on Boltzmann with the notion that organisms live by eating negative entropy (Schrödinger 1944, 72–73). He attempted to resolve the points of view of biology and physics, stressing the informatic nature of genes and hereditary transmission.

In 1948 C. E. Shannon (Shannon and Weaver 1949) introduced a measure of the information of a message generated by a sender with a probability of p_i for the ith message. This measure is proportional to $-\sum p_i \log_2 p_i$. Therefore the thermodynamic entropy and information theory entropy have the same functional form. Note the information is measured by logarithmic to the base 2, while entropy is measured by logarithmic to the base e. These are related by a multiplicative constant.

In 1957 in an important paper, E. T. Jaynes (Jaynes 1957, 620–47) was able to put together the results of seventy years. He notes that

$$I = -\sum f_i \ln_2 f_i$$

is the information that an observer would be missing about the microstate, if he knew the macrostate. Converting to log to the base e, we get

$$I = -1.44 \sum f_i \ln f_i$$

therefore

$$S = -k \sum f_i \ln f_i$$
$$= 0.693 \, k \, I$$

Entropy is thus proportional to missing information about the quantum state of a system when we know the macroscopic parameters. Thus TS, an energy, has a psychical or cognitive aspect as it deals with the observer's knowledge. He concludes, "[T]hus entropy becomes the primitive concept with which we work, more fundamental even than energy." This relation between the observer and system characterized a profound change in physics between the nineteenth and twentieth centuries.

Thus, in agreement with Teilhard, the modern view is that the Gibbs free energy has two additive components, one calorimetric and one informatic bordering on the noetic. The Jaynes paper thus validates Teilhard's intuition.

Conclusion

Examples from his essays manifest Teilhard's lifelong groping to explain the phenomenon of complexification and communication in nature that he observed. They also manifest his awareness that the classical interpretations of thermodynamics were not yet able to discuss evolution adequately. It required the insights and profound analyses of statistical mechanics and information theory. As he tried to clarify in his own mind this question of how to explain energy in evolution, he wrote in his private journal in 1951: "Question encore obscure." But his insight into how evolution takes place should serve as a lesson to those who have been prematurely critical of Teilhard's two energies.

References

Broda, E. 1978. *The Evolution of Bioenergetic Process.* New York: Pergamon Press.

Cuénot, Claude. 1968. *Noveau lexique Teilhard de Chardin.* Paris: Éditions du Seuil.

Gibbs, J. Willard. 1875–76. *Transactions of the Connecticut Academy.* III, 108–248.

——. 1902. *Elementary Principles of Statistical Mechanics.* New Haven: Yale University Press.

Jaynes, E. T. 1957. "Information Theory and Statistical Mechanics." *Physical Review.* 106, 620–47.

Page, Leigh. 1929. *Introduction to Theoretical Physics.* New York: D. Van Nostrand and Co. Inc.

Schrödinger, Erwin. 1944. *What Is Life?* Cambridge: Cambridge University Press.

Shannon, C. E., and W. Weaver. 1949. *The Mathematical Theory of Communication*. Urbana: University of Illinois Press.

Teilhard de Chardin, Pierre. 1964. *The Future of Man*. New York: Harper & Row, Publishers.

——. 1965. *The Appearance of Man*. New York: Harper & Row, Publishers.

——. 1968. *Science and Christ*. London: William Collins Sons & Co. Ltd.

——. 1969. *Human Energy*. New York: Harcourt Brace Jovanovich, 113–62.

——. 1970. *Activation of Energy*. New York: Harcourt Brace Jovanovich.

——. 1975. *Toward the Future*. New York: Harcourt Brace Jovanovich.

——. 1999. *The Human Phenomenon*. Brighton, England: Sussex Academic Press.

Notes

Preface

1.   *The Divine Milieu: Essays in the Interior Life* (New York: Harper and Row, 1960), 89.
2.   Ibid., 92.
3.   Ibid., 54.
4.   See Robert T. Francoeur, ed. *The World of Teilhard* (Baltimore: Helicon Press, 1961).

Introduction

1.   New York, 7 April 2005, *Message du Secretaire General a l'occasion du colloque des amis du Pere Teilhard de Chardin. Secretary General, Office of the Spokesman.*
2.   *Life* magazine, October 16, 1964.
3.   Chicago: Franciscan Herald Press, 1970.
4.   *L'oeuvres Scientifiques* 1:421, 1971.
5.   Cuénot, Claude. *Teilhard de Chardin*, trans. Vincent Colimore (Baltimore: Helicon, 1965), 17.
6.   Ibid., 160.
7.   Ibid., 386.

Chapter One

1.   This lecture is adapted from chapter 1 of my book *Purpose, Evolution and the Mystery of Life* (Kitchener, Ontario: Pandora Press, 2005).
2.   Vaclav Havel, *Civilization* (April/May, 1998): 53.
3.   Steven Weinberg, *The First Three Minutes* (New York: Basic Books, 1977), 144.

4. Richard Feynman, *The Meaning of It All: Thoughts of a Citizen Scientist* (New York: Perseus Books, 1999), 32.

5. See E. F. Schumacher, *A Guide for the Perplexed* (New York: Harper Colophon Books, 1978), 18ff.

6. Daniel C. Dennett, *Darwin's Dangerous Idea: Evolution and the Meaning of Life* (New York: Simon & Schuster), 1995.

7. For a fuller picture there is no substitute for reading Pierre Teilhard de Chardin, *The Human Phenomenon*, trans. Sarah Appleton-Weber (Portland, Oregon: Sussex Academic Press), 1999.

8. Pierre Teilhard de Chardin, *The Prayer of the Universe*, trans. René Hague (New York: Harper & Row, 1973), 120–21.

9. See especially Teilhard de Chardin, *Activation of Energy*, trans. René Hague (New York: Harcourt Brace Jovanovich, 1970), 97–128.

10. Ibid., 238.

11. Teilhard de Chardin, *The Future of Man*, trans. Norman Denny (New York: Harper Colophon Books, 1969), 39–63.

12. Ibid., 75.

13. Teilhard, *Activation of Energy*, 116.

14. See, for example, Teilhard, *The Future of Man*, 64–84, 129–44, 255–71.

15. Ibid.

16. Teilhard, *Activation of Energy*, 126–27.

17. Ibid., 239.

Chapter Four

1. Plotinus, *Enneads*, V, 1, 2; English translation by Elmer O'Brien, *The Essential Plotinus* (Indianapolis: Hackett Publishing Company, 1986), 92–93.

2. Gregory of Nyssa, *On the Holy Spirit Against the Followers of Macedonia* [Eng. trans., *Gregory of Nyssa, Nicene and Post-Nicene Fathers*, 2nd series, vol. V (Grand Rapids, MI: Eerdmans, 1953), 320].

3. Ibid. [Eng. trans., 319].

4. Gregory Nazianzen, *Oratio*, 31 [Eng. trans., *Gregory Nazianzen, Nicene and Post-Nicene Fathers*, 2nd series, vol. VII (Grand Rapids MI: Eerdmans, 1955), 361].

5. Ibid.

6. On the history of the concept of the World Soul, see Tullio Gregory, *Anima Mundi* (Florence: Sansoni, 1955), 123 ff.

7. Ibid., 126. Gregory points out that in making this correlation the theologians at times fell into expressions that smacked of subordinationism.

8. Ibid., 15–16, 41 ff., 123 ff. See Peter Dronke, "L'amor che move il sole e l'altre stelle," *Studi Medievali*, 3rd series, 6 (1965), 401–13.

9. Dronke, op. cit., 339 ff.

10. William of Conches, *In Boethium*, cited I Gregory, op. cit., 15; see also Dronke, op. cit., 410.

11. Dronke, op. cit., 410; Gregory, op. cit., 133 ff.

12. William of St. Thierry, *Epistola de Erroribus Guillelmi de Conchis*, *Patrologia Latina*, 180, 333–40. On the condemnation of Abelard, see *Enchiridion Symbolorum*, ed. Henricus Denzinger-Adolf Schönmetzer, 32nd edition (Rome: Herder, 1963), 722 (370). See Gregory, op cit., 411–13. The force of the objection of William of St. Thierry was directed against the technique of appropriation and the vestige doctrine. Yet this tradition continued to flourish in the thirteenth century.

13. Teilhard, "L'Ame du Monde," in *Écrits du temps de la guerre*, 221–32 [Eng. trans., "The Soul of the World," in *Writings in Time of War*, 175–90].

14. Teilhard, *Writings in Time of War*, 182.

15. Ibid.

16. Ibid., 183.

17. Ibid.

18. Ibid.

19. Ibid., 186–87.

20. Ibid., 183.

21. Teilhard, *Le phénomène humain*, Vol. I of *Œuvres de Pierre Teilhard de Chardin* (Paris: Editions du Seuil, 1955). Trans., *The Phenomenon of Man*, revised edition (New York: Harper and Row, 1965).

22. On the question of evil in the world, see Teilhard, *Le phénomène humain*, 345–48, trans., 311–13; *Le milieu divin*, Vol. IV of *Œuvres* (Paris: Seuil, 1957), 71–102. Trans., *The Divine Milieu* (New York: Harper and Row, 1960), 45–68.

23. Rabanus Maurus, *Veni Creator Spiritus*, *Patrologia Latina*, 112, 1957:

Veni, Creator Spiritus
Mentes tuorum visita.
Imple superna gratia
Quae tu creasti pectora.

Chapter Five

1.   It is interesting that the first modern scientific theory of evolution—that of Lamarck—was itself linked to the philosophical value of enlightenment: a *moving toward* progress, which became the metaphysical framework of Lamarck's evolutionary theory (see Ruse, 1996).

2.   See, among others, the letter of 27 March 1916. The letters are published in Pierre Teilhard de Chardin et Jean Boussac, *Lettres de guerre inédites* (Paris: O.E.I.L., 1986). Jean Boussac made a copy of his letters to Teilhard and sent them to his wife. This book is of great importance: It is one of the few cases where we have both letters from and letters sent to Teilhard; Teilhard never kept the letters he received. And, interestingly, Teilhard refers to Angela da Foligno in his *Journal* entry for 5 October 1916 (Teilhard de Chardin, 1975, 123).

3.   See for this aspect, and for a general discussion about the science of the biosphere and the Gaia hypothesis a paper on theoretical aspects of evolution, Ludovico Galleni, *Aspetti teorici della biologia evoluzionistica*, 1998.

4.   Recently the proposal of a new research program in theology related to Teilhard de Chardin's vision of the cosmic Christ was published by Gustav Martelet (Martelet, 2005).

5.   See again, L. S. Senghor (1962). Of interest is the fact that in a further paper (Senghor, 1968), he uses the term *symbiosis* to describe the relationships inside the Noosphere.

Chapter Six

1.   25 March 1924, "My Universe," in *Science and Christ*, trans. Rene Hague (New York: Harper & Row, 1965), 37–85. Hereafter referred to as *MU*.

2.   *The Divine Milieu* (New York: Harper Torchbooks, 1965). This work was first published as *Le milieu divin* (Paris: Éditions du Seuil, 1957). Teilhard wrote it in 1926–27. Hereinafter referred to as *DM*.

3.   *MU*, 37–38.

4.   *MU*, 38.

5.   *DM*, 45.

6.   *DM*, 43.

7.   Ibid.

8.   *DM*, 46.

9.   See Steven Weinberg, "A Designer Universe," *New York Review of Books*, 46 (Oct. 21, 1999), 16. Also *Dreams of a Final Theory* (New York:

Vintage Books, 1994), 241–61. E. O. Wilson, *Consilience* (New York: Vintage Books, 1999).

10. See Arthur Peacocke, "Science and the Future of Theology," in *Evolution: The Disguised Friend of Faith? Selected Essays* (Philadelphia: Templeton Foundation Press, 2004), 159–85. Also David Griffin, *Two Great Truths: A New Synthesis of Scientific Naturalism and Christian Faith* (Louisville, KY: Westminster John Knox, 2004). Also Charley D. Hardwick, *Events of Grace: Naturalism, Existentialism, and Theology* (Cambridge: Cambridge Univ. Press, 1996).

11. *DM*, 46.
12. *MU*, 39
13. *DM*, 46.
14. *DM*, 43–44.
15. *DM*, 112.
16. *DM*, 114.
17. Schmitz-Moormann, 44.
18. Schmitz-Moormann, 45. See *MU*, 45, 70, 74, 77, 82.
19. *MU*, 75.
20. *MU*, 75–76.
21. *DM*, 61–62.
22. *DM*, 152.
23. *DM*, 59.
24. *MU*, 44.

25. Karl Schmitz-Moormann (in collaboration with James F. Salmon), *Theology of Creation in an Evolutionary World* (Cleveland, OH: The Pilgrim Press, 1997), 28. For Teilhard's use of the term, see *DM*, 46, note 1; 128–31.

26. Wolfhart Pannenberg, "Problems between Science and Theology in the Course of Their Modern History," *Zygon: Journal of Religion and Science* 41 (March 2006): 105–14.

27. *DM*, 60.
28. *DM*, 60–61.
29. *DM*, 106f.
30. *DM*, 108.
31. *DM*, 109.
32. *DM*, 110–11.
33. *DM*, 62.
34. *MU*, 59.
35. *MU*, 67.
36. *MU*, 68.
37. *MU*, 77. Teilhard's italics.

38. *MU*, 64–65.
39. *MU*, 65.
40. *MU*, 77–78

Chapter Seven

1. A letter sent from Peking to Abbé Breuil on July 12, 1941, was not received until July 5, 1945. In past centuries the Chinese characters for "Beijing" had also been transcribed "Peking" or "Peiping."
2. Institute of Vertebrate Paleontology and Paleoanthropology.
3. To Mgr Bruno de Solages, July 11, 1941.
To Abbé Breuil, July 12, 1941.
To Ida Treat, August 5, 1941.
4. Letter to P. A. Valensin, SJ, dated Sarlat (Dordogne) August 22, 1925.
5. To Rhoda de Terra, October 6, 1939.
6. Unpublished.
7. Teilhard lists as reference the 1911 edition of *The Principles of Scientific Management* by Frederick W. Taylor.
8. "Mystics" was for Teilhard just a field of knowledge, as is "physics," or "mechanics," and so on. This meaning is carried through the entire paper. "Mystics" is meant in the sense of "intense search for God and consecration of all human forces into this search."

Chapter Nine

1. This essay is based on a contribution by the authors that was published in *Zygon: Journal of Religion and Science*, September 2005, 721–23, with some changes and additions.
2. Professor Morowitz gave the following personal historical perspective at St. John the Divine Cathedral to 750 people on April 9, 2005, about the origin of this contribution: "This is a rather personal story of a forty year unfolding of my understanding of Teilhard and Thermodynamics. I first met Teilhard on a bookstand in Grand Central Station, while waiting for a train to New Haven. The paperback version of *The Phenomenon of Man* was on sale and having heard of Teilhard I welcomed the opportunity to read a major work of his on my train ride home. Things have never been quite the same. In retrospect, what I learned was that biology consisted of a series of emergences leading to

'complexification.' This was fifteen years before I started working on complex adaptive systems. Teilhard's prescience never ceased to impress me. A few years back I wrote *The Emergence of Everything*; in a curious way Teilhard was my mentor.

"I have a long standing interest in thermodynamics in biology and was pleased in the section, 'The Numerical Laws' to find Teilhard discoursing on the first and second laws of thermodynamics. A surprise followed when I came to the section describing two energies radial and tangential. Subsequently I read several of Teilhard's critics condemning this notion. From time to time I tried to resolve the two energies problem and was led to the Gibbs free energy with its two terms, one enthalpic and one entropic. Some years later I began a dialogue with Father James Salmon in which we re-examined the two energies problem. One direction led to the work of E. T. Jaynes on information theory and statistical mechanics. Jaynes demonstrated that the entropy of statistical mechanics which is equal to the entropy of thermodynamics is proportional to the information theory measure of the information we are missing about the microstate of a system if we know its macrostate. It was a measure of our ignorance and thus had a noetic character as was required by Teilhard's radial energy. A second direction was to examine Teilhard's writing along with Nicole Schmitz-Moormann, who is editing Teilhard's works. This provided insights into Teilhard's energetic intuitions and his lifelong efforts to bring together philosophical and scientific perspectives. It was important for him to accept the coherence of the universe and the necessary unity in our ways of looking at the universe."

3.   An obvious example of early English mistranslations of Teilhard's works was *man* to translate Teilhard's French word *humain*.

4.   A detailed analysis in English by James F. Salmon of Teilhard's intuition regarding matter is in press in "Teilhard's Law of Complexity-Consciousness" in *Revista Portuguesa de Filosofia*. A thorough appraisal of Teilhard's writings on Urstoff is found in Karl Schmitz-Moormann's *Physik, Ultraphysik, und Metaphysik* (Köln und Opladen: Westdeutscherverlag, 1956), 156–57.

5.   Teilhard uses the French word *dégradation*, not *dissipation*, to portray the constant increase of disorganized energy (entropy). *Amorized* may be defined as "the activation during the course of evolution" (Cuénot 1968, 40). *Calorized* is a word coined by Teilhard to portray the increase in entropy.

6.   Omega for Teilhard can be looked at under two aspects: "1) under the aspect of emergence, a center defined by the ultimate con-

centration of noosphere upon itself; a natural point of convergence of humanity and consequently of the entire cosmos; a term of the social and spiritual maturation of the Earth. 2) under the transcending and preexisting aspect, Omega is one of two visible poles of God, that is to say God as end of creation acting by mediation of Christ-Omega. In fact both poles of God, Alpha and Omega, beginning and end, coincide with the divine unity and eternity" (Cuénot 1968, 138–39).

The Contributors

John Farina is a professor of religious studies at George Mason University. The former editor-in-chief of *The Classics of Western Spirituality* (Paulist Press), *The Sources of American Spirituality* (Paulist Press), and *The Spiritual Legacy Series* (Crossroad, Herder and Herder), he has written widely on the Catholic spiritual tradition. His current project is a book on religion and civil society, entitled *The Intelligible Sphere: Religion and Civil Society in the 21st Century*.

James Salmon, SJ, is a professor in the chemistry and theology departments at Loyola University Maryland and a senior fellow at the Woodstock Theological Center, Georgetown University. In 1982 he cofounded the Annual Cosmos and Creation Conference, which was inspired by the writings of Teilhard de Chardin. He continues as the director of the conference.

John F. Haught is senior fellow, Science & Religion, Woodstock Theological Center, Georgetown University. He was formerly professor and chair in the department of theology at Georgetown University. His area of specialization is systematic theology, with a particular interest in issues pertaining to science, cosmology, evolution, and ecology. He is the author of numerous books, including *Making Sense of Evolution: Darwin, God and the Drama of Life; God and the New Atheism;* and *Christianity and Science: Toward a Theology of Nature*.

Thomas M. King, SJ, now deceased, was professor of theology at Georgetown University. He was author of *Sartre and the*

Sacred and numerous books that explain the thought of Teilhard de Chardin. With James F. Salmon, SJ, he edited *Teilhard and the Unity of Knowledge* (Paulist Press) and was a cofounder of the Annual Cosmos and Creation Conference.

Mark McMenamin is professor of geology at Mount Holyoke College. He has written extensively on Precambrian geology, the Ediacara biota, and the Cambrian explosion. Mark's research was featured in the nationally televised History Channel program "How the Earth Was Made."

Ewert Cousins, now deceased, was professor emeritus of theology, Fordham University; general editor of the World Spirituality series; editorial consultant of the Classics of Western Spirituality series; a translator of Bonaventure; and an author of numerous books, including *Christ of the 21st Century*. He was a former president of the American Teilhard Association and a member of the Pontifical Council for Interreligious Dialogue.

Ludovico Galleni is a professor of general zoology in the University of Pisa and invited professor of evolutionary biology in the Pontifical Gregorian University in Rome. His main experimental interests are devoted to the studies of chromosome evolution and speciation in animals. From a theoretical point of view, he investigates the general theories of evolution and Teilhard's contribution to the biosphere theory.

Philip Hefner is professor of systematic theology emeritus at the Lutheran School of Theology at Chicago and former editor of *Zygon: Journal of Religion & Science*, from which he retired in 2009 after serving for twenty years. He is author of *The Promise of Teilhard* (Lippincott, 1970) and *Religion-and-Science as Spiritual Quest for Meaning* (Pandora Press, 2008).

Nicole Schmitz-Moormann, along with her late husband Dr. Karl Schmitz-Moormann, was designated by the Teilhard family and the Foundation Teilhard de Chardin to collect and edit Teilhard's scientific writings and to edit and translate into German his private journals. She has served as visiting fellow at the Center for Theology Inquiry at Princeton and as research fellow at the

Woodstock Theological Center at Georgetown University, where the Schmitz-Moormann collection is housed.

James W. Skehan, SJ, is emeritus professor at Boston College and emeritus director of the department of geology and geophysics at Weston Observatory. His research has been mainly concerned with the geology of New England, Europe, and Africa in the context of assembly and breakup of supercontinents through time. He has also focused on the geological and paleontological research of Teilhard.

Harold J. Morowitz is Robinson Professor of Biology and Natural Philosophy at George Mason University. He studies biogenesis, the thermodynamic foundations of biology, and has had a long-time interest in the philosophy of biology as developed by Teilhard.